OLUWATOYIN M.

ALMOST 40

NIGERIA | UK

First Published in 2024

Text copyright ©2022 Oluwatoyin M.
The moral right of the author has been asserted.

Kepressng (KEP) has no control over or responsibility for any author, third-party websites, or articles that may be referred to in or on this book.

A CIP catalogue record for this book is available from the Nigerian National Library & the British Library.

ISBN: 978-978-60784 -8-9 (Paperback)
ISBN: 978-978-60784 -9-6 (E-Book)

Typeset by Kepressng Ltd
Cover design by Agnes Kay-E
Cover image © Canva.com

To

This book is a tribute to women's struggle to be seen
above societal expectations by their triumphs, not just
their pain.

ALMOST 40

1

Folake Awolowo's agemates were married. Some with kids old enough to call her 'aunty,' but Folake was rather occupied with work. Her mother, Mama Rere, as everyone often called her, for being super generous and always giving towards others, would keep reminding her. Contrary to that belief, she wanted a family of her own more than anyone else, she believed, but she wasn't going to sit on her hands while she waited.

At age thirty-nine, she had accomplished many more feats than any of her female friends would ever dream of. She was somewhat proud of it; the vacuum of her singleness stared back with each achievement. There was a sweet, condescending flaunting that most of her agemates did – the waving of their ring fingers, touching their second or third baby bump demurely, or the exaggerated discussions that floated around their children's milestones. She had the perfect response – the rich aunty with the coolest gifts.

In a society like hers, being a married woman with children was well respected, making her a pariah amongst her peers, i.e., the 'ugly duckling.' Mama Rere's generosity didn't expand or stretch to patience for her only daughter's difficulty in bringing a husband home to start a new generation.

When it came to interior design, Flair and Design was one of the best in town and had even won multiple awards for their astounding performances, so it only makes sense that she got the government contract without any backing. Some had speculated she used some kind of voodoo or she was having an affair with a government official, which got her the contract. They may have seen her work portfolio and what her company had done in the past before giving her the task.

She was thrilled to receive a phone call from the Commissioner for Works and Infrastructure, declaring her the bidding winner; the three others had heavy backings and were all married compared to her. She had just secured a deal with the Lagos State Government to do the interior design for the newly built international airport, and the project was a long-drawn battle amongst four candidates, including herself, and the rest were hoping to seal the deal by all means necessary. She wanted to flaunt it in their faces, but that might seem rather too standoffish.

A big project like that required all her attention and focus. Folake had left the office for a meeting with her executive assistant and so on a regular basis, she would attend meetings with the stakeholders and government officials who were as interested and dedicated to the project as her. It was to be launched sooner than expected, but because of the rumours flying around about the project, there were doubts about the funds and the chance of finishing the project, with the keen belief that it was a ploy to divert funds yet again.

She noticed Emma, her personal assistant turned sister, fidget with the seatbelt soon after she slid in the backseat of her Range Rover. She planned to pour herself a full glass of wine as soon as she got to Flair and Design. Flair and Design, her brainchild, was set in an impossible six-storey building that housed most of her wares in the heart of Lagos mainland.

She caressed the documents on her lap, thought of calling her mother, and sighed. She remembered her mother's snotty chagrin when she took her mother to its opening a couple of years ago.

"You don't need this. You need a man." and then add her new favourite - *"If a woman is too successful without a man in her life, she would be nothing in people's eyes."*

It was what must have evolved her relationship with

Emma, who at the moment was still fidgety.

"Emma," she murmured.

Emma jumped.

"What is it? If you needed the loo you should have said before we left," she exhaled. "We'll soon be at the office."

"It's …" Emma cleared her throat noisily. "It's your mother."

She straightened.

"She's fine," Emma added quickly, stretching a handout. "She's in the office."

She let out an exasperated sigh.

"Ṣadé has treated her to Ibrahim's promotion cake."

"Order another cake," she said, smoothing a hand over the documents again. She should be celebrating this win with her mother, but it would become another knife her mother would use to stab her.

"Make it three."

Emma raised a brow, covering the mouthpiece of her phone.

"The cake. Make it three."

"I understand," Emma murmured.

She shook it off and chose gratitude. She was putting food on people's tables. She paid the best salary compared to her competition. She had everything she wanted, except a husband.

As the Range Rover drove into the reserved lot of

Flair and Design, her mother's favourite statement crossed her mind again. She tried to build a wall in her mind to shield her from the upcoming onslaught. She'd been avoiding this and had suspected it would backfire.

"We're here," Emma said, the car door on her side already opened with Emma's back arched, waiting.

"Ṣadé said she's not in a good mood," Emma said politely.

When has she ever? That woman never rests!

She exhaled. She wanted to say, 'What does she want this time?' but she knew in the way Mama Rere's smile turned to a scowl the instant their eyes met that she was better off silent. She growled in silence and rolled her eyes in her mind. Her head began to feel hot soon after.

"Should I inform Sadé to tell her that you will return late?" Emma asked in a whisper.

"That won't be necessary," she replied, although not too sure herself. "Let's just hope she won't take too long today."

"Maami, good afternoon," she said cheerfully, surprising herself.

"Mmm," Mama Rere mumbled.

They walked in awkward silence. While she nodded to her employees' greetings, her mother smiled her response until they reached the elevator. She touched her forehead and didn't lower her head until they got to her office on the top floor. She regretted her decision to come straight to see her mother.

She wished that a call would come through at that moment. Any excuse to avoid her mother, but it was rather late, and there was no going back. She took a deep breath, exhaling in chunks. She barely gathered her thoughts when Mama Rere went to her side of the desk and sat down on the pink leather laced with soft fur; it was specially customized with an orthopaedic, massager and was relieved her mother didn't know the settings.

"Maami, what would you like – "

"When are you bringing a man home?"

She closed her eyes. *This is worse, she didn't even wait to be served.*

"When will I see my grandchildren?"

She exhaled and stared at her awards, drowning her mother's words and finally said: "Maami, when the time comes, you will also celebrate with me!"

Mama Rere frowned, shaking her head in disappointment. "When is that time? When I am already dead? Or when you're in your fifties? Tell me, Folake! You will be forty in coming months, still no man, no child of your own. Do you want to disgrace me among my friends? Mrs Olasoji just gave her last daughter out in marriage, I came straight from her court wedding, and that girl is by far younger than you."

Her mood went from blank to sad. She was trying hard to maintain a steady relationship with her mother, and with men. But the men always ended up jilting her.

The one she recently broke up with didn't want to take things further than the bed; he just loved that she was hard-working but didn't see her as wife material.

"Maami, it's not my fault that men use me and dump me. Maybe something is wrong somewhere. Or someone is just doing something to make me unhappy! But I can promise you Mommy that I want to be married with children too," she finally said and added hopefully, "Perhaps it's *village people*."Afterall there was no reason why she wouldn't be married by now, when it was her dream from a young age to have her own family.

"It's not someone doing something to you. It is all your fault! God forbid bad things in your life," Mama Rere said forcefully. "You're the one that has no time for men, you're always busy chasing after wealth and material things, wanting to be like a man!"

She scoffed. Her career had made life easier for them all. Her father retired as a school principal, and her mother, having never worked, served her reverend pastor and their church. Her career changed their status in society, including where they lived and the cars they drove; all of a sudden, it wasn't enough for her ever-complaining mother.

"Maami, I'm doing something extraordinary at the moment. Your daughter just got a contract from the State government, a big project at that, but that's not enough for you to be proud of me?" she fired back.

"Ehh Folake! Stop deceiving yourself!" Mama Rere

snapped, waved her hand as she got up and, in a sterner voice, continued, "Just bring a man home and shut your enemies up! You don't need all these achievements. You're a woman. Find yourself a man who will be doing that on your behalf."

She gawked at her mother, dumbfounded.

Bringing a man home right now wouldn't be possible even if she had to hire one.

"I don't have time to go on dates," she mumbled and bit her lip.

"If you can't bring a man home, at least get pregnant by one. I don't care if he is already married to someone or is poor. All I want to see is you being with a child this year," Mama Rere insisted.

She blinked, trying not to shake her head and to keep her voice in check.

She was already tired and her head throbbed. This time, it was about childbearing. She had wanted to see and hold her grandchild even if her daughter wouldn't bring a man home.

"Go and get pregnant. You're not a young lady anymore. In fact, your days of becoming a mother are numbered," Mama Rere exhaled deeply and touched her bangles. "And before you start having problems with getting pregnant, find a man. I don't care if he is a mechanic or a fisherman. Get pregnant before the end of this year!"

Her legs weakened so she had to lean against her desk. She had never witnessed this part of her mother – another woman's husband, if possible. Any man? No man?"

"Is that what you want, Maami?" she asked, eyeing her mother suspiciously.

"Yes," Mara Rere replied firmly.

"Ok then, be expecting! I will make sure I get pregnant by any man and have his child if that is what you want," Folake sighed, not sure of what to make sense of what she was agreeing to, but she was desperate to breath even if it meant taking on the challenge her mother threw at her.

"Is that all?" she asked, watching her mother adjust her headtie and swipe the edges of her lips.

"Yes! That is what I want," Mama Rere coolly and left.

2

Folake slid to the floor, still bewildered by what had just happened, what she had agreed to, and with whom. She crawled to the cabinet that held the gifts that were given to her. She regifting stash, she pulled out a bottle of Brugal Andrés and stared at it for a long time.

She needed one after being put through stress. Over the years she had developed the urge to drink away her stress from work and life in general. Her go-to was wine. She'd been told that she drank like an alcoholic. Drinking made her sane, and without having it in a day she wouldn't feel alright. The fear of reaching forty without being married scared her to death even though she had done a good job of concealing it.

She stared at the drink and wondered if it was one of the expensive ones – Emma would know – but she didn't want to talk about her discomfort. Emma called the drinks in this drawer drinks for the 'big boys' she considered herself one in a sense but couldn't stand the smell. She needed the eerie happiness wine offered but she'd chosen to stay clear until she'd finished all the pre-prep meetings to due with the government contract.

She took the bottle to her lips and wrinkled her nose. Unable to tolerate it, she pinched her nose and took a gulp, coughed and stared at it.

Get pregnant before the end of this year.

Getting pregnant at the age of nineteen was her biggest punishment, and the worst of everything was that her so-called sweetheart was nowhere to be found. She heard he left to continue with his studies overseas. He didn't tell her. It wasn't even in their plans. Not when he bade her goodbye on the same night he left Nigeria. How cruel could a person be?

For weeks she walked around aimlessly, avoiding her parent's gaze. After two failed attempts at suicide due to cowardice and clumsiness, her mother found out. A resounding slap to open her deaf ears and blind eyes to the reality of her naivety was her mother's first response.

"This baby must not be the reason to hold you back in life," Mama Rere said after a long, gloomy silence.

Her righteousness fast-every-weekend mother, suggesting an abortion. In fact, she forced it upon her. And from where Folake stood, she'd lost the right to object and so she complied. Who would have thought that her 'church-going' Christianity-rep knew the way to an abortion clinic?

In a cold semi-dark room she lay on a thin bed with her legs spread apart, tears formed in her eyes as 'a not so nice' doctor stood over her, poking and prodding while she sucked in pain. It ended really quickly, but she almost lost her life because of the complications afterwards. She bled. Fearing she might die, her mother adorned her prayer fire. Miraculously, she survived, and till that day, she never forgot the face of the man who betrayed her.

He was Folarin Davies.

Folake patted the bottle in her hand as recalled the tall looming frame of Folarin Davies, the first boy she met who didn't have a broad nose, his brown skin glossed by the sun like melting chocolate as he came out of a forest green Land Rover.

She took another gulp from the stout bottle and wondered how life could have been different if just one man had intended to marry her. Could she have been scaring them away as her mother supposed?

The first man that ever made she believe in love also taught her heartbreak. Eighteen, a young fresher at the

University of Lagos. Her passion for design led her to study architecture, a course that required creativity and precision. To her parents, especially her father, she was a star because she went to his alma mater. Nothing else mattered to her then but maintaining good grades. She hardly kept friends, never attended campus parties, nor did she violate herself like the rest of her female peers.

But Folarin Davies, whose charming smile left her giggly, walked into her life and befriended her, and everything changed.

Intoxicated with love, her mind was polluted with every one of his smells, and her imagination ripened with the thought of becoming his. He was somehow naughty, more of a playboy that every campus girl crushes on; strangely, he only liked her.

Why her? Many of them had questioned. She wasn't the most beautiful; in fact, she was just normal, very normal-looking. Back then, she had suffered severe acne on her face, yet he was so kind to her, listened to her worries, and even protected her. He never asked her out, but she did, and he said yes. She would give the whole world to him, and he wouldn't mind either, as the two became inseparable. They renewed their affirmation of love by exchanging many kisses, and he was the first man she knew. She didn't regret him being her first. It was meant to be.

Days went by, months turned into a year, and they were still together. Happy and in love, walking hand-in-hand to lectures on dates that she had sponsored with the money she was supposed to use for herself.

Her heartbreak came slowly. She made excuses for him, forgave him all the time, and gave him her body all the time, even when she didn't feel like it. Even when it started affecting her academics, she went from being a straight-A' student to getting a D at most. The once so-proud parents became her biggest critics, advising her to sit up tight or risk getting carryovers. Still, she was being blinded by love until she realized everything was a lie.

If she had known then that she was the purser of the relationship, could she have stopped?

Folake sniffed, shaking her head. Her mother had touched a nerve she obviously had forgotten. *Go and get pregnant. Could this be the same woman, or did desperation blind her to the scandal? What the church would think? Or, how would the world judge her for raising such a 'wayward' daughter?*

Folake touched her stomach with her free hand, whimpered, and took another gulp.

Folake was tipsy, the bottle empty and near its nuzzle, a wet patch on her rustic handmade carpet when Emma walked up to her office, an ugly sight she didn't want to keep showing to her employees, especially to Emma, who knew of her alcohol violation. The flustered expression on Emma's face made her comport herself, hurryingly to hide the bottle, but Emma had seen it all.

"Ma, why are you drinking again? I told you not to worry about anything. Everything will be fine!" Emma consoled pitifully, but consolation was not what she needed at the moment, not even pity, as she was nothing but embarrassed to have been caught.

"Emma, you are married, right? Also, you have your own kids?" she asked abruptly. Emma nodded 'yes', but was still confused by the sudden interrogation.

"How does it feel like to be a Mom?" She asked.

Emma's face lights up when discussing her two adorable kids under five. She was still in her twenties, but she had been married and happy with children. "They're the best thing that has ever happened to me. They're just amazing and fill me even on sad days."

"That's why I'm going to have mine!" she blurted out. Folake hadn't been so serious about anything in her life, but this time, she was dead serious about the decision to have a child of her own.

"Ma, are you getting married?" Emma was excited to hear the good news but got relaxed when her Boss said otherwise.

"But how are you going to get pregnant?" Emma asked. She probably wasn't aware that one needed to sleep with a man in order to get pregnant, it doesn't matter whether you are married or not, pregnancy could happen. She must have thought so since she got married as a virgin.

"I don't need to be married, Emma. I just need a man, more like a donor!" Folake replied. Her intention was to find a sperm donor that met her requirements so she could conceive. She had thought of several ways to get pregnant, but finding a donor would be the safest method to go about.

"Where are you going to meet such a man?" Emma pondered, still confused about her boss's crazy intention.

"Through an audition!" she blurted out after a short silent pause.

"I'm sorry! Did you just say audition? Like we should audit men for sperm donation?" Emma was flabbergasted. Folake was also aware that there was nowhere in Nigeria where men would gather for an audition to get a woman pregnant when there wouldn't be any sexual inter-relationship between the two. If it were to be something sexual, many men would gather even for free, but not when they have to go through medical measures just to get a woman pregnant artificially.

"I don't think that will be possible. It is better to be in a relationship than to go through such measures! Why don't you try dating again?"

"I do not want any relationship with the father of my child that's why I'm doing it artificially. Plus, I'm ready to pay whatever just to get his sperm!" she explained. Having and raising a child by herself was what she hoped for now, not to share the custody of her own child with anyone else.

"Do you think men are going to show up?" Emma asked, amused. "As sperm donor?"

Emma nodded. "It will be like a work interview."

She paused thoughtfully and shook her head.

"Any guy that passed with flying colours will be initiated into the talk and agreement!"

Emma blinked, crossed her arms and frowned.

She sighed with relief, almost smiling. She could do this single-mother thing, at least she had the money to care for her own child.

"So we are to deceive these men?" Emma said dauntingly.

She let out a loud burp and covered her mouth.

"I'd like us to start immediately. Speak to HR, but don't give them details. Come up with something."

"Do you think this a good time with the project at hand?"

She waved Emma's words away.

"Emma, you're making me look like a weird person here. My mother just left after threatening me to give her a grandchild this year. So, what am I supposed to do? I can't farm a man. I can't get pregnant on my own. Most importantly, no man would want me for a wife." Tears trickled down her cheek as she finished her statement without realizing it. "I'm desperate. Very desperate."

"Ok, we will do as you want. Just know that I'm still

not one hundred percent sure this is the right option for you. But I love you, and I want you to be happy." She professed, enfolding Folake in her embrace. Emma had always been the only one Folake could trust on private matters; she knew that the moment she made Emma her executive assistant.

"Thanks for understanding me, as always. Now, I need to sober up and get back to work. Can you please tell Femi to see me in my office? I need an update on what he is working on." Instantly, her passion for work fueled up, and she was ready to bounce back. Luckily, she was the type that couldn't get drunk easily; she would need more alcohol before reaching a tipsy state.

"I haven't seen him at all today. I heard he hasn't shown up to work.," Emma replied.

"Just imagine that. Now, my mother would think I'm the wicked one if I fired him. It is my fault, I shouldn't have employed him in the first place," she rambled. Femi was her cousin, and she had employed him because of her mother's persuasion since he was fired from his previous job and would have to make a living in order to feed his family. Even though Mama Rere saw her daughter as someone doing a man's job, she wouldn't hesitate to ask for favours for her friend's children from Folake, and she had done most of them favours by finding suitable employment for them.

"We really don't know what he's up to these days. All

we know is that he has a sweet mouth and is never afraid to use it," Emma said as she bent over to whisper to her. "I heard him and Winifred are in some kind of affair or something."

"Winifred and Femi?" she exclaimed. She took a short pause, then continued. "Tell Winifred to see me in my office."

"Ok, ma. Please, don't say you heard it from me," Emma pleaded. She was a good friend of Winifred, but also loyal to the core to her boss.

3

Folake was now out of her depression. More work needed to be done and she would be travelling to London in a few days to get some materials that were not in the local market. She had contacted her dealers some weeks back and they had confirmed to have such in their possession. She was getting some cold water to drink when Winifred knocked on the door.

"Come in," she said as Winifred stealthily entered. Oblivious of what brought her over, she offered her seat after drinking some cold water that fully woke her up.

"Miss Winifred, I have been hearing some rumours about you and Femi at work. They said you are both in some kind of affair. Which shouldn't be since Femi is a married man, and he is also my cousin."

Winifred suddenly became uneasy, and she could tell she was aggravated by her insinuation. "Ma, I'm sure it was all a rumour. I'm not in any relationship or affair with Mr Femi. We are only friends," she clarified, although her body language tells otherwise.

"Is that right? Because there shouldn't be any of such going on here. This is a respectable firm, and I don't want any scandal to happen, not when we have a big project at hand," she admonished. Even though she had become suspicious of the two, she decided to take Winifred's word for it since that was what she also wanted to hear.

"How is the budget analysis coming up?" she intercepted.

"It's about to be completed, ma. We've added enough buffers and some necessary adjustments to it. By tomorrow, it will be on your table," she assured, maintaining her composure as much as possible.

"That's good. Tomorrow, you will be following me to the Ministry. We are going to present the budget analysis to them so we can get the mobilization fee first. I can't be using funds from my own pocket to do government work." She had heard rumours about some government agencies owning money for years, and that shouldn't become her portion.

"Ok, ma. Is that all?"

"Yes, you may leave."

A sense of relief was felt on Winifred's face upon hearing her dismissal, and she left in haste.

4

Folake was driving home, clocking out for the day when she decided to branch off at a local market to get some ingredients needed to prepare the vegetable soup she had been craving for days. Now she needed it more than ever, not when she had been put under stress, and all it took was her mother's visit. Even though she wouldn't be the one preparing it, she still wanted to help by getting the ingredients needed. While her house was located on the island, her office was on the mainland, which was closer to the local market that sold each of her needs at a cheaper price.

Three years before, she bought a four-bedroom

duplex mansion in Banana Island, the wealthiest neighbourhood in Lagos. The property cost a whopping four hundred million naira, and she also owned a Range Rover with the latest Mercedes as her car collection. She was not a fan of sports cars, so she never invested in one. She was a big girl who needed big cars after all. She had two other people living with her: a steward who took care of the house in her absence and a cook who made her some special delicacies whenever she wanted. On the weekend, she would have a cleaning agency come over for deep cleaning, including the moderate-sized pool she hardly used since she wasn't a fan of swimming, she only liked it as an aesthetic.

Apart from being ridiculously rich, She would still price down whatever was expensive in the market. After all, she was a businesswoman. A meat seller had called a ridiculous amount for a price on something someone else might have paid little for, all because he saw her driving a Range, he wanted to quickly cash out, not knowing Folake knew how to play the game well.

"Ah ah, Oga! Wetin? It is five thousand Naira. How can I buy this for ten thousand? That's too expensive! Please cut the meat for me abeg," she complained, even the seller was taken aback by her confrontation.

"Haba my customer, everything is now expensive in the country. Dollar is now expensive," he spoke with a thick Hausa accent. He was still holding the knife, hesitant to start butchering the meat, while trying so hard to convince her to do his bidding.

"But no be dollar we dey spend for Naija now. If you cannot accept my price, let me go somewhere else." Some other meat sellers were ready to poach her to their side, wooing her with decent prizes which made him change his mind suddenly. He immediately compiled with what was on the ground, or else he might lose a potential customer. He agreed to sell it to her for five thousand and even patronized himself. He told her that whenever she needed to buy meat again, she should always come to his store, and she promised. Folake did the same with the tomato seller who wanted to raise the price of tomatoes but later changed her tune to what Folake proposed.

She was driving out from the Market when she saw a depressed young man who couldn't hear her horn several times, so she decided to park near him and genuinely took interest in his worries. His melancholic, sombre appearance made her interested in knowing his worries; strangely, she wasn't the type to be intrusive of other's business, but something in her needed to know why he was sad. One could tell he had trekked a distance judging by his dusty feet, and disgruntled appearance.

"Young man, why are you so lost in thought? Don't you know you could get into an accident?" she asked sternly.

He immediately apologized.

5

"Are you going somewhere? Can I offer you a ride?" Folake asked.

She frowned at the sense of familiarity she felt near him but she was certain she hadn't met him before. She could almost feel his pain as if it was her own, weirdly enough she had never met him before.

He was quiet, and staring at his hands.

"Come on, let me be of help. Where are you going?"

He hesitated and then said, "I'm going to the city hospital, ma. And it's still far from here," he said solemnly and shyly.

"It's okay, I can help." She had left the area and

turned into the main road but would still gladly offer to give him a ride regardless. He entered the front seat, fastened his seat belt, and she made a quick turn towards the direction she had left.

While they were stuck in traffic, she wound down the window and stared at the visor for a while then asked, "Are you visiting someone in the clinic?"

"My mother is very sick!" he said in a groggy voice, staring at his hands.

"Oh! I'm sorry. How is she coping?" she asked out of concern. It took him a few seconds for him to give a reply because it was heavy in his heart to say.

"Ey ya! That's very sad. How much is the money needed?" she asked, concerned.

"It's five million naira, Ma. There is no way I can find such an amount of money, even if they sell me, I can't come up with such an amount. We have looked everywhere, no one is willing to help us."

"What if I help you out? Would you mind?" she offered. It was not in her position to give out such money, but she had more than enough, so she could spare.

"Ma?" he exclaimed in disbelief, a couple of emotions, crossed his face. "You want to help me? I don't even know you, you don't know me, but you still want to help me? Even my own Uncle had forsaken us, but you want to help?"

"I am willing to be of help to your family. What's

more important than saving her life?" she said to him and gave him her 'trust me' smile.

"To prove it to you, why don't we go to the hospital together?" she suggested. "Right now?"

"Yes, right now. I have some time to spare if you don't mind."

He swallowed and nodded.

"Thank you ma. I don't even know what to say at the moment. I just want to be sure that this is not a dream. Or am I dreaming?"

"You're not," she replied, still smiling. They soon arrived at the hospital, and without any further deliberation or 'let me think this through'.

She made the payment for the surgery. The nurses were shocked because they weren't expecting him to come up with such money.

Filled with joy and gratitude, he prostrated on the floor and eulogized her.

She had the money to spend anyway, and it came from her heart to help him. But he was embarrassing her, and there was nowhere to hide, so she bent down to lift him.

"It's okay. Please can you get up from the floor? It is so embarrassing. I was just doing my part and now it's left for the doctors.

He obliged happily and hugged her but she stiffened and gently shrugged him off.

"Here is my card, do let me know if I can still be of help!"

"Aunty, I can't thank you enough. I don't know how I should repay you for your favour. God will bless you indeed!"

She drove home. With everything going on in her life, seeing the happiness of others eased her worries, and she hoped God might remember her one day. If there was one thing she had in common with her mother, it would be that both had good hearts and put others' needs first.

That night, Mama Rere called again, reminding her about their previous discussion. She told her not to joke with her words by letting them skip her mind. "No matter how busy you are, get a man to impregnate you," She admonished yet again.

"Mommy, I already told you I will work on it! In fact, I'm working on it," she reassured her again. Folake wasn't joking when she promised to have a child of her own; this time, she would do it to surprise her parents, who had their own doubts.

"Don't let it be like last time. I don't want to later find out that you're just leading me on. Go and get pregnant!" She strictly warned again.

"Mommy, I have heard you. Is that all?"

"That's all. Good night!"

She sighed loudly after she hung up. She made up her mind to visit the hospital before the weekends. The next thing on her agenda would be to get her ovaries prepared for childbearing. The gynaecologist she visited two years ago said her ovaries were in good condition, and that she should not take too long trying for a baby.

She shook her mother's counsel off and tried to come up with a plan for the next two weeks, plans that were crucial to the airport project. She'd always been meticulous about her work and life, everything around her must be perfectly done before the appraisal, and she knew she had to lead by example so others could follow.

She also went through a catalogue from an overseas supplier, examining the cost and materials she was to pay for before her travelling. This supplier were the few she paid in advance for because what she saw in the magazine was almost always what she got.

One thing she detested the most was getting stressed overseas, not when she would need some alcohol as a dependent to shake off her worries, and that might be unprofessional of her which may even get her into trouble.

Every item sent to her was what she needed and she paid for it through her domiciliary account. As that was done, she went to take a quick shower, she didn't like taking long in the bathroom, and in haste, she returned to watch her daily drama streaming on TV. She fell asleep while watching the thirty-minute play on her big flat screen; thankfully, she dozed off in her own bed while

OLUWATOYIN M.

the TV played in the background.

6

After two failed payments, Folake called Femi but was unable to reach him and decided to call Emma. She sent him several messages to him but he didn't answer. She had never been so embarrassed, so she called Emma but was unable to reach him either, as he hadn't shown up to work since she left. She hated the complication of using her domiciliary account but had run out of options when she discovered that her favourite supply was low on stocks that were in high demand.

By the end of the first week of her shopping, she was desperate.

"Emma," she responded impatiently to Emma's greeting. She missed most of what Emma had to say except the fact that Femi said he didn't answer her. She couldn't believe what she had just heard.

"He told you that?"

She had known in her mind that she shouldn't give him the position of accountant. But Femi was family and her mother had nagged her day and night. If only she had taken Ijeoma's advice and added an accountant so she would have someone to fall back on.

"Yes, he did," Emma confirmed.

She was stuck. There was nothing she could do now. She would have to return to her shopping when she sorted the finances. She also realized that moment that she needed to put a stop to his flaring ego, she had accommodated him enough, and it was time to let him know who the real boss was.

Three days later, on a hot Monday morning, she was escorted by Emma to the fourth floor, a surge of rage built up in her as she alighted from the elevator, marching directly to his corner.

"Femi," she called politely.

She knew he was ignoring her because she was right beside him. She called him a couple of times, trying to keep her cool as he was much older than her. But she was done, so she spun the chair so he was facing her, and Emma turned off the computer.

"You're fired, Mister Femi."

"Who do you think you are?" Femi replied with a chuckle.

"Go to HR and ask for your two-month advance salary," she responded, surprised that she was calm.

"You cannot fire me," Femi said with a wave of his hand.

"I don't want to see you step foot in this enterprise henceforth."

"See this small girl o! Do you think you're talking to your mate?" Femi asked, getting up and tucking his hands in his pocket. Everyone present watched in awe as the reality unfolded in their eyes.

She blinked in surprise at his outright arrogance. She had been patient enough in accommodating his shenanigans, and she had reached a point where she could no longer spare him.

"Femi, I don't want you anymore in my enterprise. Get your things and leave right away."

"Just because you run a company like a man doesn't mean you have the right to be talking to me in such a manner. I'm still a man, older than you. Have respect for your elders and apologize right now before I change it for you."

She scoffed. Even the people present were whispering amongst themselves, mocking Femi because of the ridiculousness that came out of his mouth. He was using seniority to prove his sexist nature. He had been like that since day one, always exuding his toxic masculinity side to prove his worth.

"I should apologize for disrespecting you. Maybe I would if one day you have a company as big as mine," she air-quoted her words sarcastically.

Femi's composure faltered but a few seconds.

"Abeg, stop showing off for this people, you can't fire me," Femi shouted.

Minutes later, she called for the security team to escort him outside, and they didn't hesitate to bundle him out when he refused to leave.

He kept shouting as he was being dragged out, cursing and threatening her but she didn't care at all. Firing him was much easier than she had imagined, but the only thing she feared was the fact that her mother would react negatively if she heard, and she was right.

Just as she reached her office, she received a phone call from her mother. Femi had apparently called, swearing over the phone, but Mama Rere had entertained such behaviour towards her own daughter, only to confront her for firing her dear nephew.

"Folake, what has gotten over you? Why would you disrespect your older brother and even sack him from work?" Her Mother lashed out on the phone. She was over the top and was screaming her lungs out.

"Mommy, you can't decide how I run my company. I fired him from his job because he deserves it," she explained, even though she didn't have to.

"Well done, Miss Company Owner. Are you the first person to own a company? If you had owned the world, what would you have done?"

She kept sighing as her mother continued.

"Don't you know that Femi is older than you? Why would you treat him that way?"

"Mommy, just because Femi is older than me doesn't mean I won't talk to him anyhow or fire him. I'm the CEO, regardless of what you think of me. He is a man, after all, he shouldn't be working under a woman. Tell him to get a job somewhere else."

"Folake, all this pride won't get you a husband. No man would want a woman that puts pride first, you need to humble yourself," Mama Rere said.

She knew instantly that if she didn't put a halt to their conversation, her mother might waste the precious time she had left before the meeting, so she ended the call without saying her goodbyes.

Fortunately, Winifred walked in at the right time, and they left for the Ministry.

7

Folake presented the updated design to all stakeholders from the Ministry. As all stakeholders nodded in agreement, she remembered Mama Rere, Femi, and the number of men in the room. Apart from her and Winifred, there were no women with significant authority. Even if she were to give up, most of her employees have stayed as long as they have in the industry because of her doggedness. Should she give up now because of her mother's belief?

Her focus returned when Winifred got up to brief their audience on the budget analysis.

The leader of the government parastatals, the

Commissioner for Work and Infrastructure, finished his statement with the promise of half of the funding before the commencement.

She stiffened, squinting at his white flowing agbada and almost nodded, but she had carved a niche in a male-dominated industry not to be a pawn. The commissioner exuded the pride Femi had, and she wasn't ready to be bullied yet again, so she said:

"That's fine, but we need to have a contract that binds those promises. I will work on it and send the draft to the office," she suggested.

She wasn't worried about the look of disbelief that they wore. She assumed they they she was disrespecting them. Winifred seemed to want to distance herself from her and it made her wish she had come with Emma who had a doctor's appointment.

"Are you looking down on the government that awarded you this project?" the commissioner finally said. " Or don't you know how lucky you are?"

"Certainly not, sir. I just want both parties to agree so there won't be a cause for argument in the future."

"It's okay," the commissioner said a long while later. "We will do as you have suggested. Draw the memorandum and send it to my office sooner."

Soon after the meeting, she turned on her phone. It was as if the god of war had more in store for her because her mother's call came in but the commissioner insisted she went to lunch with him so she didn't pick up the call.

Unlike the rest of her life, the design was perfect, and the team was ready. The commissioner turned out to be quite understanding of her stand. He mentioned he wanted to introduce someone to her, and she was curious to meet this person he had spoken highly of.

"He was the one that made me think twice before giving you the project. He said he knew you would do a fantastic job if given the chance."

She didn't like the direction of the conversation because she had assumed she got the project on merit.

"I can't wait to meet this person, because I know my connection didn't reach politics," she said as she gave an uncomfortable smile. They were already at a reserved restaurant, waiting for this person and were yet to make an order.

Some minutes later, a man in a dark blue pin-striped suit walked toward her and took a seat adjacent to her.

"Hello, Folake. Nice seeing your lovely face again," a voice said.

She looked up and almost peed on herself. She looked at his extended hand and at his face and blinked. She got up slowly at first, gave an excuse, and made a quick exit.

At that moment, she was panicking; her heart was pounding heavily, and she wished she could disappear before he reached her. Her legs ran faster, and she arrived at her car. As she struggled to find the car key in her bag, he was coming towards her direction, trying to be friendly to her.

Fortunately for her, she found her car key sooner, entered it, and drove away while this stranger kept calling her name. She watched him through the rear mirror, and he was still standing—the same Folarin that she knew and couldn't forgive easily.

Folarin! What does he want? she wondered, clicking her fingers and shaking her head.

It was a Saturday morning, and Folake finally made it to her gynaecologist.

She would be travelling the following week to finish the transactions Femi had caused her to abandon. She had to sort out the childbearing part first. Deep down, she was scared that her eggs might have become too old, but she had some fate in her that she would become a mother one day. A series of tests was conducted on her. A transvaginal ultrasound was done to examine her ovaries, as well as blood tests to check her hormone levels. Her blood pressure was high due to stress, but she was advised to take things slow.

"Miss Folake, your body needs rest. We can't start this process without you being at ease," the doctor said.

Apart from her blood pressure, everything was normal. The doctor even commended her eggs as fertile and young, and she may not even need the artificial process to get pregnant.

"Why do you need to go through the IVF? The test results show you're well and capable of having a child of your own."

"Doctor, I'm not married yet. And I don't think I would be the future. But I would love to have a child of my own before it is too late," she said. She felt it was right to be honest but somehow unsure if there would be discrimination against her decision.

"That makes sense. I have seen some older women who have done the same, even younger women are not left behind these days. I guess the world is changing."

"Doctor, I want to know if I'm breaking any law here. Do you think it is suitable for me, as a single woman in Nigeria, to get an IVF?"

"There is no law at the moment that stops you from getting an IVF as a single Mother. You're old enough to make decisions for yourself, and it's commendable enough." The doctor paused for a moment, took her eyes away from the screen she had been staring at and asked a candid question. "Are you seeking a donor? Or do you want the hospital to provide one for you?"

"I am seeking one myself. I want to be the one deciding the fate of my child," she replied with much confidence.

"Ok then, that's fine. Do come back with the donor whenever you're ready. We can commence the process, but I have to warn you that it might be a long one. So, are you ready for this challenge?"

Folake gave a deep sigh. She somehow knew what she was getting into, and was ready for it. "I'm ready, Doctor," she said confidently. She was even surprised that all her alcohol intake wasn't a problem hindering her from getting pregnant, all that was required was to get enough rest.

She had to share the news with Ijeoma when she called at the right time as was leaving the hospital. Ijeoma was a very good friend of hers who had become her best friend over the years. Most of the friends she grew up with, and the ones she went to the university with had abandoned her right after they got married and wouldn't invite her over to their homes or their gatherings.

She had also hated being around them before she realized she was no longer wanted. Every time they gather, they don't usually have more things to discuss apart from husband and children talks. Only Ijeoma had stayed glued to her. It was three years ago Ijeoma's husband moved his family out of the country to Canada for better opportunities, but Ijeoma still hadn't forgotten she had a friend back home. Both would constantly call each other and talk for hours non-stop.

"Hey best friend, I have a gist for you," Ijeoma said on the phone before she could break the news to her.

She was curious about Ijeoma's excitement and knew her friend could talk, one of the best things she loved about her. She had her put on speaker, as her ears listened while her eyes concentrated on the road as she drove home.

"I heard Felicia is getting a divorce," Ijeoma broke the news.

She almost shouted in disbelief. It can't be the same Felicia she knew, the one that always put marriage first before any other thing and had shunned divorce.

"What happened? What did her husband do? Why is she getting a divorce?"

"More like what she did. Her husband caught her cheating, now they are getting a divorce."

It was confusing for her to comprehend. "So it wasn't her husband, but her?"

"Yep! And not just one, but two. She has two boyfriends. It was Comfort that called last night to give me the full gist. Who could have thought that the same Felicia, the holy one that always preaches marriage and lifestyle on social media could be getting a divorce?"

"Haba na, have mercy on her. She could be going through a lot at this moment," she said with concern.

"Don't tell me you have an ounce of sympathy for the same woman that spoke ill of you? Or don't you remember when she was mocking you for being the single one amongst us?"

"Of course, I remembered. But she was the only one that had the courage to confront me, the rest only talked behind my back. But why worry when I have you, you stood up for me that day and put them in their places. You don't know how reassuring that was."

It was like yesterday when Ijeoma blasted those women who thought they were better off than Folake, but the only thing they had going on for them was their husbands and children.

"Of course, I will do it again. Tell me, what do they have? They should have been grateful for all the money you've spent on them. I'm sure they can't afford a cocktail anymore now that you've left the group. Arrogant women, so full of themselves."

She laughed out loud. She was already halfway home.

"Bestie, your girl is getting an IVF," she finally declared.

"Oh, my days. Folake, I'm very happy for you. That's a bold step to take, and I'm glad you're finally getting the experience of motherhood."

"Well, I'll be having a child through a sperm donor," she explained.

"This is hooge girl!" Ijeoma exclaimed and began to hoot.

"I know, right?" she said, smiling. I don't want the hassle of sharing custody of my child."

"That's fine. I agree with you one hundred percent. Men these days can be annoying. I'm just happy that you are finally going to be a Mother. My friend, Motherhood will look good on you."

Ijeoma was the right person to break the news to and she knew that she would be as joyful as she was. Even though it was the pressure that led her to make that decision, she still wanted someone to celebrate with her, and Ijeoma was that person for her. It was also the confidence boost she needed.

8

Another call came in during Folake's conversation with Ijeoma. It didn't seem to be in her contacts, but she thought it could be from work since anyone could call her line at that moment. She ended their conversation with a promise to call her back when she got home, and it was at the time she was about to pull up in her estate. Only for her to answer the call, but she turned out to be the person she was avoiding at all costs.

"Hi, Folake. It's me, Folarin," he spoke with a deep, manly, loving voice.

Immediately, she ended the call without further

questioning. She felt an eeriness after hearing his voice again. Their union ended many years ago after his betrayal, but now that he was back in her life, she felt stabbed in the heart.

She drove into her compound. Mr Aleshinloye, her butler, was the one who opened the gate for her. It felt like yesterday when their paths crossed. He was going through a mental phase after losing his only grown son and wife to a fatal car accident. Thinking the world was ending for him, she came into his life and brought him home so he wouldn't think of committing suicide and since then, he started working for her and had also become a fatherly figure to her.

"Are you alright?" he asked, concerned.

"I'm fine sir. I just need some rest," she said softly; both knew she wasn't fine, but it wasn't something to drag on for long. Folarin's call had made her unwell all of a sudden. Even after her doctor had told her to take things gently, the thought of Folarin had gotten on her nerves. Mr Aleshinloye helped her with her bag and led her into the house. She asked her to cook to prepare her favourite salad and bring it to her room, she wouldn't be having dinner. She was on a diet before, but somehow felt she needed to be physically fit than ever.

She stood in front of a mirror in her room, examining her body, and the thought of not being beautiful enough clouded her mind. She was neither thin nor too fat, she was of average weight with a good body proportion.

Suddenly, her stomach felt too big for her.

"Why does he have to show up now?" she muttered to herself while staring at her own reflection in the mirror. She was thinking about Folarin, her first love. He was the one that made her feel good and also bad at the same time. A painful scar he had left in her heart and body and she wouldn't forgive him easily.

"What does he want now? Where was he twenty years ago? What does he want from me after everything?" she muttered, pacing and clenching her fist.

She felt anger, loss, pity, and disgust at the same time. She would have to talk to him at some point, but she wasn't ready to face the truth of his betrayal. The cook brought the salad she asked for, and she instantly devoured it in haste. She later asked for Amala and ewedu soup because she got hungry.

9

On a Sunday morning, Bimpe, Femi's wife, had called Folake over for an urgent discussion. She wished for them to meet after Sunday services, and after the early morning Sunday school, she drove to the mainland to visit Femi's family, ignoring Mama Rere's persuasion to meet their reverend who had something important to tell her. According to Bimpe, Femi hadn't been home for a week now. She got hold of the news of her husband's layoff from her own mother-in-law, and somehow, they made it her fault. She had no other choice but to appease Folake to give Femi a second chance.

"Aunty Folake, maybe if you give him another

chance, he would probably come home. The children and I haven't seen him for a week now, and he didn't leave any money for their feedings," Bimpe pitifully said, almost in tears. She was a wreck, and her home appeared to be just as her state of mind. The children looked unkempt and grumpy, and one could tell they hadn't been eating well. Folake knew well enough to have brought some foodstuff with her; she had always done so whenever she visited. Even the three children loved having her around and wished they could live with her. And it was the first time Folake ever noticed Bimpe with scars that appeared as a result of domestic violence.

"Did he hit you? Has he been hitting you all this while?"

"No, I just fell," Bimpe lied.

"Bimpe, for God's sake, stop covering up for that man. He has no respect for you or for the children. You left your banking job to be with a man who has no future, and you make him lord over you. That's the problem!" she lectured.

She frowned at Bimpe. Bimpe was a great asset, but Femi had manipulated her to believe she was otherwise.

"Can't you leave him?" she asked suddenly, although worried how Bimpe might take her concern for her.

After hearing that, tears formed around Bimpe's eyes. She became emotional as she hugged Folake. She was vulnerable and weak, and the person she needed the most was Folake to have her back.

"Aunty Folake, I want to leave him too, but I don't know how. I don't know how to ask for a divorce because I fear he might hit me again. I don't even have the money for a lawyer," she cried out.

She felt her pain. She had taken Bimpe as a sister ever since she got married to that douchebag of a husband. There were times she wished Bimpe had stood up for herself, but now, things have changed.

"Don't worry about getting a lawyer. I can always arrange the best one for you. But first, we need to get a restraining order from the court. We have to separate the two of you. Are you up to the task?"

Bimpe nodded. She has had enough of being misled and abused by both her husband and his family. It was time she took care of her own life and children.

"I need the four of you to come home with me. I have rooms to accommodate you for the time being, and when you start working, you can move out," she proposed. The children were the happiest upon hearing they would be living with their favourite Aunty, and couldn't wait as they left for their room to start packing some few belongings.

"I can't thank you enough, Aunty Folake. God will bless you," Bimpe prayed.

They left with her, and all had left their past behind them. She didn't hesitate to contact a lawyer on Bimpe's behalf, and he promised to get Bimpe a divorce without worries. The evidence was there already, Bimpe had also confessed that Femi was dating his coworker, to which made her angry as Winifred had blatantly lied to her, her action causing pain for the person Folake cared for.

"When did you discover he was cheating? Because I asked Winifred and she told me it wasn't the case, that they were good friends."

"Good friends? She had no respect for me or the kids whatsoever. She just paraded herself around with that ingrate, and they flaunted it as if they were some married couples."

"Paraded? You've met with her?" Folake was stunned. The Winifred she knew was different from the Winifred Bimpe was familiar with.

"Yes. Paraded. Even his mother knew of the affair." Every word of Bimpe sounded like a bomb to her ears. To think her Aunt knew of the extramarital affair and still chose not to do anything spoke so much of her character.

"The aunty I knew would never condone such a thing for her own daughters. What is going on with these people?" But if her aunt knew, could her own mother also know of the affair but keep quiet about it? she wondered.

"Do not worry. I will deal with those two myself. I promise you that they would both be on their knees asking for your forgiveness," she reassured her.

Even though she wouldn't be in town for a week because of her trip to London, she had to seek personal security for the family staying with her, just in case Femi showed up to harass them in her absence.

10

Folake had to delay her travel after two of their local suppliers reported cutting ties with them all of a sudden. The news brought about the impromptu sourcing for a new supplier, and she had to stay behind and monitor the task. It was disappointing that these were suppliers she had maintained a serious business connection with over the past, only for them to end up disappointing her when she needed them the most.

They also had to arrange to source talents to collaborate with outsiders since they had other smaller projects to work on apart from the state government task. Hiring new designers was expensive, but hiring part-time would suffice. There were already seven head interior designers, including her, the CEO, and two architects who had been working for quite a while and had become family.

Emma texted shocking news to her while a meeting was happening. She was in the conference room with the head designers, holding a discussion about the final draft of the design, which had been finalized by the stakeholders since she wanted everything to be perfect and done right before leaving for London. Emma spoke with fear, reporting that Femi was outside the company's premises, threatening to commit arson. He appeared to be drunk and had both a lighter and petrol at hand as he screamed her name. Two security men who could have held him down and handled the situation were avoiding him since he posed a threat.

"Call the witch out now! Call the home wrecker out," Femi shouted, drawing the attention of people passing by to stop minding their business and rather gather around to watch as it unfolded in their eyes.

She knew it might result in this if he ever found out about his wife's staying with her, but how he got to know of the divorce sooner still baffled her as well as it concerned her deeply. Folake had urged Emma to call the police while she stepped outside the premises to confront Femi.

"Ma, he's not joking. He might really set this place on fire. I'll advise you not to go out to see him. Let the police handle things," Emma worried, holding her by hand to prevent her from moving continuing her walk to Femi.

"It will be fine. Just call the police," she pressed, withdrawing herself from Emma's grip. She went downstairs to confront the situation; she was unafraid, and nothing scared her about a wailing dog screaming her name.

"Did you ask Bimpe to divorce me? Are you the one putting ideas in her head? Just because you cannot find a Man of your own, you have to destroy another woman's home." Femi ranted. He was unstable as he wobbled like a drunk. The security men urged her to stay far away from him so as not to provoke him further, but she had no fear in her whatsoever as she got closer to him. She found him to be worthless in her presence and was in his worst state ever, so she took pity on the woman who had been married to him for years.

"What a shame, Bimpe deserves the world and more. You're just not the right one for her," she said.

"You're dying today, bitch. Today is your last day, so you had better say your goodbyes," Femi shouted. He began to open the small keg he had brought with him, the one containing the petrol, and started splashing it everywhere.

A part of it touched her body, but she was unbothered. The security men who could have saved the situation were afraid of getting involved, but they couldn't stop him no matter how hard they were screaming and threatening Femi, warning her to leave the scene before things got out of hand. Everyone watching from afar and the employees spying through the windows thought it was a better option to stay away from trouble but worried about their boss, who was still outside with a potential killer.

As he was about to switch the lighter, a gentleman rough-handled him from behind, snapped the lighter from his hand, and brought him to his knees. It was then She became conscious of what could have happened. Her life was almost endangered, but somehow, she had not skipped a bit to make a run for her life.

She gasped for air; her vision was blurry for a moment, and as she was about to collapse to the ground, the gentleman held her in his arms while the Police, who had come on time, arrested Femi, and he pounced on the police car. Soon after, the police car's siren faded, and she realized that the person holding her was Folarin.

11

Recovering from the shock of finding Folarin at her doorstep, Folake quickly pulled away from Folarin's embrace; the last person to be holding her would be him.

"Are you okay?" he asked, looking concerned.

Folarin, with raised brows, asked, "Why did you stay and watch him almost hurting you?"

She grimaced. Hearing him was already hurting her.

Folarin gestured at the security guards. "And they should also be fired for not doing their jobs right."

Even though she wasn't happy with how her security guards handled things, she wouldn't like Folarin of all people ordering her about, much less her employee.

"Don't tell me how to run my company," she scolded Folarin.

"But I'm only looking out for you," Folarin said in a familiar soft voice. "The worst things could have happened if I hadn't come looking for you."

"If I die or live, how is that any of your concern?" she mumbled. She roused to her feet and let Emma guide her back into her office.

Moments later, better composed, she prepped herself to leave for the police station to file a complaint and possibly press charges against Femi. She promised herself not to forgive him easily for his crime regardless of what anyone thought or suggested, most especially her own mother, who could come or call anytime.

She had temporarily forgotten about Folarin until he took a seat adjacent to her. She squinted at his audacity. He seemed too comfortable in her presence, something she hated him for.

How dare he? Who does he think he is?

"You don't seem too happy to see me," Folarin said arrogantly.

You think? she thought as she sneered at him, smoothing his hand over the lapel of his jacket.

"It would be weird if I had welcomed you with open arms," she sarcastically replied. His action irked her. It was as if he was oblivious to what he may have done to her twenty years ago.

"To be fair, I was expecting that. After all, we used to

be an item in the past," Folarin said, basking in a smile. His fresh, ever-delectable smile that made her fall for him in the past reminded her of nothing but a toothpaste advert.

"What do you want, Folarin? I don't have all the time in the world to spare for you."

"I'll be in town for a while now before heading back to the States, and I think it will be lovely to have you show me around town."

Show you around town? "Do I look like a tour guide to you? Or do you think I have the time to spare for you?"

You're still the same self-centred, cocky, and ego-driven Folarin that believes he still holds my mumu button.

"Come on, don't be like that. I just want to spend some time with you, you know, like the old times when we were in school."

She kissed her teeth. "Old times indeed."

"That's fine. I'm still around for a couple of months, we can always make time for each other."

She wasn't sure if he was too pompous or naïve to think she would want to go out with him after everything. She wasn't ready to talk about the past, but it still annoyed her that he was oblivious to what he did to her. She told him she would be leaving for London in two days, so she wouldn't be available to take him out or even spend a minute with him.

"Listen, Folarin, you're probably a married man with

kids, just because I'm still single doesn't mean I will stoop so low to philander with you. I don't even have the time." She dramatically picked up some files and stubbed them on her desk.

"Maybe God is punishing me for leaving you. I was married with two lovely kids that are my world, but sad enough I can't even see them anymore as their mother had issued a restraining order against me."

"I didn't know that," she murmured. Feeling sorry for Folarin, she asked, "What happened?"

"She just proved to me why I should have married my kind. I lost everything, Folake. My home is gone. My car. I was fired from work because of her. Now I'm back in Nigeria and in your presence. How funny is that?"

She felt sorry for him but wouldn't forgive him that easily. She would listen to his worries, but not welcome his advances. After all, he was only here because everything went bad for him.

"So have you forgiven me?" Folarin asked eagerly.

Folake reluctantly nodded.

"When will you be back in Nigeria?" she asked, almost eagerly.

"I'm not going for long. I am going there to get some stuff, and I'll be back after that."

They talked for a long time, and The two talked for long in her office before Emma came with the news of Winifred submitting her resignation letter and left for good without saying a word to her boss. She had confronted her in the morning when she arrived, and she had confessed to dating Femi who had shown no interest in her lately.

"Did she leave with her paid salaries?" she asked.

"She did. The problem is that we need to fill her position as soon as possible," Emma said worriedly. Scouting for talents might be easier, as it was hard for them to find people that match their working energy.

"Don't worry, we will find someone soon," she promised.

"And how about the other audition? The sperm..." Emma covered her mouth.

"That will be later, Emma. You may take your leave." Embarrassed, Emma briskly walked away.

Did he hear... did he understand? She wondered nervously as she watched him press his phone. She looked up at the time and almost exhaled in shock. *Femi. The police station.*

Folarin raised his head with a smile on his face when she began to shut down her PC but she pretended not to notice. She let him join her at the police station where she gave her statement. Luckily he was the eye witness she needed, even though she tolerated his exaggerated explanation of how life-threatening it had been and bloatedly labelled himself the hero. It was a good thing Folarin came to because they began to play the gender card. For Folarin's sake, Femi was not granted bail.

It was as expected. Mama Rere had dropped by to wail about Femi's arrest, definitely not about the crime he committed against her one and only child. Seeing Bimpe and Femi's children riding around the compound on the bikes she'd bought them seemed to have angered Mama Rere even more.

Thankfully, Bimpe wasn't home.

"You cannot keep living this way, Folake. Stop meddling in other people's business." She enunciated her words very slowly and carefully. She had come with a driver, and as dark as it was it didn't stop her from coming to confront her daughter.

"Mommy, what is it again? What have I done?" she asked, tucking her hair in a bonnet.

"You've done everything in your power to destroy the life of your cousin," Mama Rere ranted.

I see you chose Femi over me again.

"Not only did you destroy his home, but now he would have to spend some time in jail just because of you."

"Mommy, were you aware of the fact that Bimpe's life stopped just because she married that useless Femi?" Mama Rere hissed and undid her scarf. "That woman gave up everything, including her job, to be married to him; now see how he has repaid her. With constant beating, and he wasn't even faithful to her."

"And so what? Isn't that the sacrifice one makes for marriage?"

She gawked at her mother. "Mommy?"

"How is that a big deal?"

She gasped, her anger rising and her chest tightening.

After all, I'm also married," Mama Rere boasted, adjusting her *bubu* with pride.

"The same sacrifice you made to be married to daddy?" She inhaled sharply, her voice shaking. "Is that what you're proud of? Mommy, I watched you live an unhappy life just because of marriage, but here you are boasting of a toxic home in my presence."

She held her breath to keep her lips from shaking; her father was not overtly caring but was averse to extra-marital affairs. Mama Rere never confronted her husband on the matter of his infidelity even though none of his past affairs was unknown to her but went to great lengths to please him and then wept all night whenever her husband left home to satisfy himself elsewhere.

She wiped her tears. "Aren't you filled with anger? I knew you cried every night because of daddy, and since I was little, I've wanted my own freedom for myself because that's the only way to love myself. I don't need a man for money or for a roof over my head. I owned the house I live in, the cars I drive, and the company I built from scratch. And it's because I wanted to become a better version of you. Seeing you vulnerable and poor and unable to speak for yourself made me rethink the life I wanted for myself."

"And so what?"

She shook her head. *You listen with one ear.* She was relieved to have expressed the feelings she had buried for many years.

"With everything you've acquired," Mama Rere continued. "You still don't have a man to call your husband."

Frustrated, she started, "Well…" and then exhaled. *There's no point.*

"Not even a child of your own."

She let her mother brine for a while and said pointedly, "That's why I'm telling you to wait with open arms for the child. I'm already working on it. I have checked with my gynaecologist, and they tell me I'm fine. So wait till you hear the news of me getting pregnant."

Mama Rere wore a smile of joy. "So I should wait?"

"Yes, you should wait," she reassured her.

"Ok. That's fine, after all, that is what matters the most. But, your cousin, do forgive him. Let him off this time, I am sure he won't do it again," Mama Rere said quickly.

"That cannot be possible, Mommy. Femi almost committed murder and arson. It is left for the law to punish him. And for his divorce, do not concern yourself over it if you want to see your grandchild."

Mama Rere's glare softened when her eyes met Folake's.

"Ah, *Omo mi,*" Mama Rere raised her hands in

surrender. "Whatever you want. Let my sister fight her battles.

She rolled her eyes in her head, reminding herself to tell the security guard to keep everyone else out even if they came with her mother.

"Folake *mi,* I know in my heart of hearts," Mama Rere sighed, striking her chest and getting up. "You'll be the best mother in the world. Let me go and tell your father."

12

Folake left Lagos on Friday due to an issue of ticket scarcity; the airline she normally used had sold out its seats for the week and wasn't taking preorders. With her new project, she needed all the help she could get. Thankfully, Folarin came to the rescue, and she was able to acquire one without any stress. Femi had managed to get out of jail but she'd ordered a security team to protect Bimpe and her children and even filed a restraining order against him.

She arrived in London with peace of mind. It was spring over there and was slightly cold compared to the heat she was used to back in Nigeria. She was glad she had packed some extra warm clothes as spring welcomed her and chose the most convenient suite.

She would have preferred waiting to be a mother in marriage, but she had not gone on a date for a long time, and it wasn't for lack of trying. She thought of Emma's children, Bimpe's children and her mother's demand and sighed. She could have also travelled with her, but she wouldn't want to leave her children who were still very young.

Emma kept her on top of things. The surprise was that Akeem was reported to have showed up that Friday demanding to see her, but Emma had told him he needed an appointment with her before demanding to see her.

"If he ever comes around again or calls the office, please let him know that I will be around next week Sunday."

"Are you acquainted with him personally?" Emma curiously asked.

"Somehow, I happened to have paid for his mother's surgery."

"What? So you don't even know him personally, yet you paid for his mother's surgery?" Emma couldn't believe what she heard.

"That young man needed help, and I was in the position of helping him. Truthfully, I had even forgotten about him until you said he came. Tell him not to worry, I will definitely get back to him."

A lot had happened to her that she forgot about the

help she rendered to a complete stranger. She would also want to know how his mother was doing if the surgery was successful.

"How about the audition? How is that coming up?"

"I still can't believe we are doing this, but everything is under control."

"It would be like a job interview, as you suggested —"

"Ah! Yes! It's like killing two birds with one stone. It's a perfect plan since we need a new accountant for the finance team anyway."

Folake nodded, smiling. As a job interview, it would weed out gossip. And with Emma being in charge of it the looks, physique, and intelligence of the selected candidate would be more than ordinary. She almost giggled. It was dubious even for her but it was exciting as well.

She scoffed cheerfully, knowing that Emma would probably be tapping her chin thoughtfully and pacing.

She remembered a saying that God always sends someone, but she had always believed it was in regards to marriage, because it was always told about in the singles-to-be-married class. Emma and Ijeoma had shown her that God always sent people to those who had no one and she was glad that she ignored the absence of Emma's WAEC certificate and took her on board. It had caused a stir, but three of the people she'd hired at the same time had left when her business partner did.

She decided to go for a walk. She had found that she

could only do that in London. Perhaps it was because no one knew her.

After a few appraisals, she took a stroll along Oxford Street that afternoon. She liked the street because she was just one of the myriad sandwiched people. It was mild cold because it had rained, but she could manage.

Remembering the delicious food she'd tasted the last time, she decided to get on Bus 159 to Trafalgar Square, but was surprised to find that she could no longer pay cash for the ride.

"You need an Oyster card, miss," the driver had said politely.

She nodded, hiding her embarrassment and got off the bus. It reminded her of Nigeria, where nothing seemed to change, but she'd return to a street she always walked through to find that a house had blocked the shortcut.

After searching got a place to buy the *Oyster* card for ten minutes she decided to sit in a café a cup of coffee, and let the thought of being a mother swirl around her.

Maybe I can have my baby here so it can have dual citizenship, she thought. Raising a child in the UK could require forfeiting her company if they had the same rules of citizenship as the US. She hoped she'd finish the Airport project before she had a baby.

She was still in the café when Ijeoma's call came through. She had called via *WhatsApp*, and the internet was uninterrupted all thanks to the Café's wifi. She resisted the urge to Ijeoma about Folarin's reappearance and his need to invade her space but blurted almost loudly.

"Folarin showed up."

"What? What does he want?"

She wrinkled her face at the loudness of Ijeoma's voice.

"What are you quiet? Look, babe, don't trust that guy one hundred percent. God knows what he wants from you now."

"He is actually not that bad. He has been of good help to me, and I'm grateful he is around," she said quickly, playing idly with her fingers.

"Babe, don't forget so soon."

"I…" she hesitated.

"Where was he twenty years ago? I heard he got married to an *oyinbo* woman and had children with her, but all of a sudden, he returned to Nigeria to stay by your side. Girl, don't forget the -"

"I did not forget the past," Folake said quickly, almost snapping at her friend, and then softly added, "It's just that being his friend wouldn't mean a bad thing."

Or would it? The feelings she had for him had returned, but there was no trust she knew that. A part of her had warned her to be cautious. But he needed her. It wasn't like she was going to try anything with him. She'd never date a married man.

"And so?"

She closed her eyes and tried not to listen to her betraying heart. If she had a man, she wouldn't need to be a mother alone.

"Would you use him as your sperm donor?" Ijeoma asked, her voice low for the first time. Her voice was only ever low when she was worried.

She hadn't thought of Folarin in that way. She didn't want strings attached when it came to having the baby but…

"So, you don't mind sleeping with that man again?" Ijeoma asked, sounding offended.

"I won't sleep with him. Why would I want to sleep with him?"

"I don't know, probably because you've forgiven him."

She wrinkled her nose at Ijeoma's suggestion. Folarin was familiar. She didn't need money from him, she had hers. She didn't need to sleep with him because sleeping with him might mean there would be a potential relationship in the future. The last thing she needed was any sort of relationship with the man who was still going through a divorce. She thought it would be over her dead body to want Folarin, but she was no longer sure.

"Don't get it twisted, girl. You may use him, but don't let him use you. Use him as a sperm donor if that works well for you, but discard him like he did you in the past."

"Okay," she said, her shoulders falling.

"Wait... have you talked to him about what happened twenty years ago?"

"Not yet. I don't even know if I have the boldness to ask him why he left with no words. What do you think he would say?" she asked, hopeful and staring at her coffee.

"Whatever excuses he gives shouldn't be our problem. Make sure you make him feel the guilt as much as you felt in the past. He shouldn't go scot-free without the thought of killing a chance with you."

She knew she would always feel much better if she talked with Ijeoma, and as always, she had found a way out of her troubled feelings. The two later discussed other issues, including the one Ijeoma didn't finish when she last called. Gossiping made Ijeoma happy, and the best person to gossip with was none other than her. Time passed, and she returned to her hotel to prepare for another day.

13

Folake was done with her shopping sooner than expected, and it was all thanks to her never-failing dealers who understood the business and stood by their words. She would be returning with a few essentials, while the heaviest supplies would arrive by shipping in the following weeks. Her flight to Nigeria was still scheduled for Sunday; by Friday, she was bored and mostly idle, so that evening, she decided to visit a friend and mentor whom she had taken as a godfather. Bill Carson.

Bill Carson was a renowned industrialist and architect. She got acquitted with him through a mutual friend, and it was a rare opportunity for her. Ever since they were introduced to each other, they became instant friends. Working in the same industry as him got them excited, and Bill had seen her as a capable being who had been able to make a name for herself despite being a woman in a male-dominated industry. Although he retired early, he had isolated himself from the busy and bustling city of London and moved back to the countryside to an estate of old centuries that his bloodline had possessed and managed.

This was her first time visiting Bill Carson's estate, an old manor house, and he was a great host to her. Having to leave the city to come down was a gesture he appreciated, and he had made sure all his staff ensured her comfort and safety. He told her to stay over for a day, and she had humbly accepted since he may have been lonely by himself in a thousand and five acres property that he lorded over. When she asked him why he had never remarried after his wife died five years before and both never had children due to fertility issues, he just comfortably smiled, telling her that he hadn't met the one that had captivated his heart yet.

"I'm sure you will find someone one day," she assured him.

He flashed a charming smile at her. Even though he was older, his body was still very agile, and it was a fact that he was a heartbreaker during his youthful days.

"I don't know about me. What about you?" Bill threw the same question back at her; she was flustered because they had never discussed private matters until now.

"I don't know, Bill. I've been through a lot with men in the past. All I want now is my happiness."

"Do you have a specific type you go for?" Bill asked jokingly, and she was amused by his sudden interest in her.

"I don't have a type," she lied. If they were not tall, dark-skinned, charming smiles, with full-grown beards, then she wouldn't have met her match.

"Do you care about age?"

She raised her brows at his question; he was intrusive compared to normal days and she wanted to know why he cared so much about her all of a sudden.

"Well, if you don't mind, I have a younger cousin. He's divorced, and I cannot wait to introduce you both."

"You have a cousin?" she asked surprisingly.

"Yes. I don't know if you know him. He's Matthew Carson, the Viscount of Brute-Island. He's just two years younger than me, and the words of his butler are that he's very lonely these days. Maybe you both can heal each other and find happiness in each other."

"The Viscount and I?"

"Yes, I believe you're made and ready for that lifestyle," he teased.

She laughed with him, even though he was dead serious about setting her up but she didn't find herself suited for such a fancy lifestyle. Or maybe she had no confidence in herself, or maybe she wasn't ready to date outside her comfort zone or date older.

"Bill, I love the idea of being a Viscountess but I don't know about dating a Viscount."

"Why?"

"I don't know. I just think it's strange."

"You should probably think about it. Matthew is a really good guy, and I'm sure he will do his best to woo your heart. He's very handsome, you know," he flattered.

"Handsome, you say? Maybe I'll think about it," she teased.

Bill also asked if she ever showed interest in relocating to the United Kingdom, but no matter how stressful Nigeria was, she would still choose to stay. Nigeria was so dear to her heart that she wouldn't *japa* like the rest despite the struggle of operating a business in a not-so-welcoming country, not even when her mother was close by or as people judged her lifestyle. Nigeria had been a perfect place for her to grow.

"You should probably give it a try. The UK might still have an untapped market for a company like yours."

"You're certainly right, but you should know that someone who looks like me might have a hard time settling in."

"Oh, don't mind that. I can always protect you. You have my word," Bill said in a serious tone.

"Or, you just want to keep seeing my face?" she asked playfully.

"I mean every word I say."

She wondered if Bill somehow believed he had no time left and that the only person he had grown an attachment to over the years was her. He made it known, making her realize how special she was to him.

"Maybe I'll think about it now that you said I'm special." She stifled a laugh. "You know it's nice hearing how valuable I am to you. My parents, most especially my mother, never opened her mouth to tell me she's proud of me."

"She must have been a fool then."

"A fool indeed," she said and reprimanded herself.

"Why, though? Who wouldn't be proud of you? Come on, look at you. You're beautiful, successful, and intelligent. If I have a son your age, I'll have married him off to you."

She felt comforted by his words; no one had really said it to her like that. To her own people, she wasn't beautiful; she was just basic-looking because she had no fuller body that drove men insane. Even her own mother had advised her to eat a lot so she could add more flesh to her model-built body. She wasn't even classified as intelligent but considered prideful, but when he mentioned that to her, it pleased her more.

"Well, being a successful unmarried woman in the society I come from is not considered an achievement but a hindrance to finding a man."

"Nonsense!" Bill said brashly and coughed. "There's plenty of men here for you. Once you're ready to meet the viscount, just let me know. He will be fortunate to have you in his life." He sounded like the father she never had. Her own father hardly communicated with her, and their relationship wasn't the conversant type that would lead to him saying those kind words to her.

"Thank you," she said, moved to tears.

"I only tell the truth, and you shouldn't put yourself down," he admonished. She spent the night in one of the cosy suites housing one of Leonardo Davinci's expensive paintings that Bill had mentioned earlier to have cost arms and legs, the one he won from an auction and planned on gifting to her. Still, she refused to accept it as it was rather too much for a gift.

She felt transported back to the Regency era while in that room. She had always been fascinated by old manor buildings as an interior designer herself, and while in that room, she felt an attractiveness to own a building as such in the future

It would be a perfect place to raise a child in the future, she thought.

14

Bill Carson drove Folake to the airport himself. He was reluctant to let her go but had no choice. He had been used to having her around in those two days, she had stayed a day more to venture into town, and he stayed glued to her side. The hug he gave her last left a long impression on her; it felt genuine and comforting, making her feel bad for leaving him behind. She had convinced him to visit her in Nigeria, and he had promised to make that visit since he would love to go to the country she loved dearly.

"Don't worry, I'll make sure you have a good time in Nigeria," she promised him before joining the queue at the departure gate.

Before midnight, her plane landed at Muritala Mohammed Airport, and Mr Aleshinloye came to pick her up. The first thing she did upon her arrival was prepare for work, arranging for the employees from the warehouse to go to the airport to pick up her cargo, which she had organised for entry during her flight. It was something she'd learnt from Bill to prevent delay in stacking and for ease of retrieval.

It was reassuring for her to have met Bimpe and her boys in good health. According to Bimpe, Femi never called or came around. Bimpe thanked her for keeping her and the boys safe. She wanted Bimpe to resume work as soon as possible while she could because it would keep her mind and body sane. She planned on discussing it with her later in the day and would also seek employment for her through her unlimited, fruitful network.

One would think travelling a distance would have made her tired, but she had left for the office before nine, agile enough to start working again. She still needed sleep and probably more rest, but she planned on doing that after everything was settled. Her designers and contractors had to begin work before she could feel the need to take a break, and that would happen soon. Emma was there by her side as she inspected the interior of the freshly completed masterpiece, a motel-cum-resort.

Her local contractors were on site when she showed

up; she held a quick meeting with them concerning the products yet to arrive. Thankfully, it wouldn't be an issue, and they could begin work without it. The set timeline for the project should be eleven months and some days, and Folake was confident about finishing sooner. She had spoken to the architects responsible for the design of the airport, and she had also been shown both the 2D and 3D designs. She intended to incorporate four elements in her designs. She knew these elements would go hand in hand, providing a sense of modernism and sustainability.

"We must incorporate nature and balance it with a sense of adventure. Let's make every traveller feel like they've been transported to paradise," she said at her first meeting. Now, it was making sense to them. They easily caught on to what she was describing, wowed by her imagination, and even commended her brilliance.

Afterwards, she left the site with Emma. On their way, they discussed the issue of sperm donors and how early they would hold the audition. Emma suggested Friday. She had left it in Emma's care, and she wouldn't interrupt her in finding the right donor.

"What criteria are you looking for, just in case?"

With a notepad, Emma was ready to jot down all of her wants and dislikes. But she didn't really have any dislikes or likes; she needed someone very healthy and in good shape.

"What if he's ugly?" Emma asked, her face imitating a disgusting expression as she held a pen in her mouth.

"Not ugly," she said quickly. Her type had always been the good-looking ones.

"Exactly, so why are you not bothered by physical qualities?"

"Who says I'm not?" she asked distractedly.

"You are?" Emma teased, cracking Folake up.

"Seriously, if you're ever in my position. What kind of guy would you select as a donor?"

"Probably someone like Henry Cavill." Emma didn't hesitate with her reply, biting her lower lip seductively, taking her aback with her response. She further described the British actor as a beastly man in god-like form, and he was her first-ever crush.

"Just imagine. You once told me your husband was your dream man."

"He said I was his dream woman, but the feeling isn't mutual," she replied sharply, feeling overly confident. She was left astounded again. This wasn't the same Emma she knew - the lover girl who got married as a virgin and never knew any man apart from her husband.

"Would you prefer someone younger?" she asked abruptly.

She wouldn't mind the donor being on the younger side but of legal age.

"Sure then, I'll find you the fertilizer for your eggs," Emma said.

She chuckled, Emma had an uncanny way of easing her nerves.

She hadn't heard from Folarin ever since she got back from London. He only sent her a text when she arrived there but never called to check up on her ever since. Could he be waiting for her to call him as she usually does in school? She thought to herself as she took her nighttime shower.

Ever since Folarin came back into her life, she had been feeling some complicated thoughts that she may or may not have answers to. It was as if age hadn't taken over him; his youthful body and face, which many girls drooled over in the past, kept her up in the shower, arousing some sensual feelings in her. She longed for his kisses, his touches that had left some remarkable feeling of lust in her. His warm embrace that sheltered her in time of need, and his good fucking...

"Damn Folake, get your act together. He's married," she scolded herself as some explicit and illicit images of him flashed in her mind.

She quickly got out of the shower after spending over ten minutes fantasizing about this same man who left a huge scar on her heart. She was supposed to resume working on her laptop as she usually does, but suddenly felt the need to pleasure herself sexually. It had been long since someone had dealt with her sexually. And 'dealt' means how badly she wanted it but couldn't seem to afford it because of how busy she had been.

She only imagined Folarin's face, and she was now aroused. Gently, her hands trailed to her lower part, her imagination held onto his gorgeous face as she was engulfed in the bliss of sexual ecstasy before releasing the exhale of satisfaction. She had done what no man could perform by herself, but she suddenly felt embarrassed of it. She wasn't someone to self-pleasure herself; she hadn't even tried it until now, and it was all because of him, that one angel who became a daredevil in the end.

As she lay on the bed, with her phone beside her, patiently waiting for Folarin's call, she couldn't deny how desperate she wanted him regardless of everything. She wouldn't want to be the first to reach out; at least she must possess some self-control and have little self-respect for herself. Or so she thought, but she ended up leaving a 'miss you' message on his WhatsApp before sleeping it off. How shameless of her!

She expected his reply or a missed call but there was nothing. He hadn't even read the message she sent which was upsetting her. Wasn't he the one who suggested they become friends again? Why would he now be avoiding her?

She began her practice on her yoga mat. Although she hardly finds time these days to exercise, she still made sure she did some stretching before leaving home. She set up a more upbeat tune and stretched. Just as she was settling into a pose, someone knocked on her door.

"Yes?"

"Ma," Mr Aleshinloye started. "Your mother is here."

Not again! she thought as a grunt escaped her mouth. She exhaled, moving into a cat-cow pose, saying, "Tell her I'll be with her shortly."

She reluctantly made her way down the stairs a while later, knowing her mother was there to bring up marriage babies.

When she joined them downstairs, Bimpe and her children were already at the dining table, having breakfast. She could see the fleeting looks of disgust on her mother's face whenever she glanced at Bimpe.

"Maami, good morning," she said and then frowned at the strange man her mother had brought into her house as she added, "Good morning, sir."

"Folake, we have to talk privately," Mama Rere said, practically dragging her back to the room she just left. It seemed her mother wanted to enter her bedroom with the man, so she sat on one of the steps.

She grimaced.

Please don't ruin my weekend.

"Ehen, Folake, this pastor, Reverend John, has come specifically to deliver an important message.

Here we go again.

"Let us go to your room and talk well," Mama Rere tried to walk past her, and the pastor nodded enthusiastically.

"Maami, we can talk you're here."

"Mmm, okay o!"

Her mind wandered to her 'pet project' with Emma; she had followed blindly, oblivious and expectant of what secretive conversation she was to have with her mother this early Friday morning. They had planned for this same Friday to interview these 'male job seekers' who were in the dark about what their duty and future implies.

"Pastor, please wait for us downstairs."

The pastor nodded but looked disappointed.

"Mommy, you have to say whatever is in your mind and not leave me in the dark," she initiated as Mama Rere was acting wearingly to start a conversation after all her flare.

"You see the reverend downstairs. God has sent him to you. He's here to fulfil the word of Christ through you," Mama Rere spoke calmly, and it was very much unlike her.

"Ehn ehn...what is it this time?" she replied nonchalantly. This wasn't the first time this reverend had something to deliver to her. The last she remembered, she was asked to donate a huge sum towards the development of the church in exchange for a husband.

"Don't act nonchalant. He's here to deliver you from the starvation of your husband and children. He has fasted thirty days on your behalf, and God specifically told him to follow me here this morning because he's ready to deliver you."

She blinked, gawking at her mother but Mama Rere sounded optimistic.

"Deliver me? Anyway, how much does he need this time?"

Mama Rere was hesitant to continue, and she was starting to believe the sum required might be higher this time, seeing how her mother's reluctance.

"It's not about money," Mama Rere whispered, even though they were the only ones in the room.

"So, what is it then?"

Her mother lowered her voice when she mentioned the reverend's solution.

"Maami!?" she screamed.

Mama Rere covered her mouth.

"Only five minutes. You won't even feel anything," Mama Rere said, looking excitedly.

She wasn't sure what feeling to react to as her mouth hung open - flabbergasted, insulted, disappointed, whatever feelings anyone would feel when reacting to a piece of ridiculous disgusting news. Her own mother was suggesting she sleep with the reverend if she wanted to break free from a supposed life crisis – being a wife.

"Mommy, can you hear yourself speak? You brought *that* man into my house because he suggested sleeping with me, and you think that's normal?"

"What is the big deal?" Mama Rere asked, looking

confused. "After all, it won't be your first time. He will be done quickly, and you won't even feel anything."

Is this woman normal? As if that makes things better. It was now she realized her mother was the biggest enemy of her life.

"I can't believe you, Maami."

"My dear, you look ready, just lay down' Let me go and get him."

"Maami," she cried, balling her fists.

Mama Rere stumbled to a halt and suddenly looked smaller.

"You really disappointed me this time, and before I open my eyes, I want you and that idiot gone from my house," she cried, pointing at the door.

Mama Rere glanced at the door and at her daughter.

"What is wrong with you? I'm telling you that he fasted on your behalf, and in order for the miracle to work, he has to be linked with you."

"You're suggesting I sleep with a married man who's a supposed reverend, and you think it is holy? Have you gone insane?"

"Eh! Don't talk in such a manner to your mother. Or am I not your mother?"

"Sometimes I don't think so. If not, you will not be here talking rubbish and wishing bad things for me."

She didn't allow Mama Rere to speak further before pushing her out of the room and locking the door behind her before she fell to the floor, holding her chest in her hand, fighting for air to breathe in her struggle to fight back the tears formed in her eyes. She didn't want to drown in pain, so she made up her mind to confront the two downstairs. In anger, she lashed out at the so-called reverend, who was supposedly *in-the-spirit* when she came down while her mother sat beside him, trying to pacify the reverend.

"Both of you should leave my house," she ordered. "Now."

"Folake, what is wrong with you? If you don't have respect for me, at least have some for your reverend," Mama Rere scolded, adjusting her *gele* properly. She signalled the reverend, apologizing on her daughter's behalf.

"Mr Aleshinloye?" she shouted while trying to pull herself together.

Mr Aleshinloye appeared moments later, along with Bimpe and her children were concerned.

"Drag these two out of my house. I don't want to see them here ever again," she said, demonstrating and seeing Mr Aleshinloye reaction, added, "And my mother."

She could hear Mama Rere wailing and swearing as she climbed the stairs, but she wasn't going to tolerate this new level of humiliation.

15

Folake sat on the bed, a tingling sensation on her chest, a reminder to take her hypertensive drugs. She was diagnosed many years ago to have suffered from high blood pressure, and she had accounted for it as a result of stress from work, but now it appeared that the person responsible for it was her own mother.

The first thought that came to her after the whole fiasco was to drink. She needed a shot of whiskey or vodka, but prevented herself from fulfilling that thought as she needed to *prepare* her body for a baby. She had only recently begun to link her uneasiness to whenever her mother visited or called. Apart from being her greatest critic, Mama Rere had become her greatest fear and challenge, the source of her pain, past, and endeavours that manifested as her birth mother.

She arrived at work later than normal. She wasn't in a good mood, and she became even crankier when she heard from the commissioner that morning that his nephew, Folarin, had returned to America. Of course, Folarin hadn't changed; he was the same Folarin who left without saying a word to her, only to return twenty years after disappearing.

Emma's head popped in before her body.

"Boss, Boss," Emma cooed as she walked in. The interview had been conducted in her absence and Emma was there to make a report about who she had selected as best suitable for the job.

"Look, Emma, get straight to the point," she said in angst.

"Is everything alright?" Emma asked, concerned.

"Emma, I don't want to talk about it now. Just send the person in right away," she said, frustrated, although she became remorseful afterwards.

"Sure thing," Emma said slowly, then left the room. She later returned with a familiar face, leaving her confused and wondering.

"You?" She stood up, baffled by their presence. The guy Emma walked in with was none other than the same man she helped weeks before. How could she forget him when she was thinking of him, wondering if fate would reconnect them? Baffled, she leaned towards Emma who was now beside her beaming, and asked, "What is he doing here?"

"He came here for the interview, and he passed, of course," Emma cheered, clapping her hands joyfully, but she returned the gesture with a stern, not-in-the-mood-for-play glare.

"The interview —"

"Are you being for real?"

"Yeah," Emma said and nodded.

She thought she was being pranked, but according to Emma, Akeem had turned out to be the best candidate amongst the rest. He stood out due to his physicality, an important criterion for his selection.

"Can you leave, Emma? I want to speak privately to him." She waved to a seat, and Akeem took his seat while Emma quietly walked out, leaving the two alone. Akeem appeared desperate - there was some unsettling anxiety he radiated in her presence, and she wasn't sure if he was the right person for the task, but she might as well hear him out.

"Has my assistant briefed you on what your job really is?" She scanned him with a watchful eye, judging him already with a preconceived idea of him being a desperate person because if he wasn't desperate, he wouldn't be sitting in her office out of all places. She had helped him out of free will but wouldn't like people taking advantage of her, just like Folarin had done, making her relearn her lessons over again.

"No, ma, but she asked me some weird questions that I didn't understand."

"Questions like what?" she asked, trying not to stare at his lips.

"About my blood type. She asked me the last time I had sex and if I had tested for HIV. I don't know if that matters for a job here."

"She's right. Look, here..." She was trying so hard to recall his name but realized she never even asked him before. "What's your name?"

"It's Akeem, ma!"

"Alright, Akeem. Where did you finish school?"

"College of education, ma. Graduated with second class upper," he said confidently.

"Your department?"

"Accounting, ma. Although I have never practised, you know how hard it is to get a job in Nigeria these days."

There was a sudden change in his demure, and she felt sorry for him.

"So what do you do to hold on?"

"I have a carpentry business where I run on a small scale."

"That's good. We need a new accountant in the team,

and you might as well fill the role. But there's one more important task you're employed for…" She paused, her heart beating fast, and she tried not to look silly. "We are looking for a sperm donor. I am seeking one."

He didn't flinch or show any form of disgust.

"Ok, ma, there's nothing I wouldn't do for my lifesaver," he replied.

She inhaled sharply. "Akeem, this is not something you should see as a repayment. I'll pay you for your service, anything you want just name it as long as it's in my possession. Just know that this is not a joking matter but a serious one. I want to have a child of my own, and I can't do that alone, that's why I need your sperm."

"Ma, you did what no one else could do for my family. When you picked me up on the street that day, I was coming from my uncle's place and he had told me no when in fact he has the money to help. So, there's nothing you want from me that I will not do."

She became uncomfortable but it was a weird transaction for her probably weirder for him so she concluded that moment to seize the opportunity. Besides, he may even be the right person for the job, someone who has a reason to give back to her.

"That's fine by me then, you're welcome into the company."

She smiled as she extended her hand out for a handshake. He took her hand in his, somehow his hand was much bigger than her. Overlooking his lean stature, he was tall and also muscular in his fit and definitely younger than her; she hadn't noticed how good-looking he was until he got up to leave.

"See I told you he's the one," Emma said, praising herself.

She couldn't deny it any longer. "Please, make sure he's settled in the company, and most importantly, make him sign the documents before we proceed to the next phase."

She couldn't risk him suing her in the future, changing his tune about the matter, or worst of it all, making it seem as if she had forced him to donate his sperm.

She was now feeling better. No thought of Folarin or the early morning fiasco, only the thought of the coming baby. She was eager to start working and resumed with a quick meeting with her co-designers. They mostly discussed the project at hand but got initiated into another big project that delighted her. Her company had just won another bidding, this time it was a renovation of a royal palace. She hadn't competed for this but got it because the King himself had chosen her for the job. Even though it wasn't as big project like the airport, this would also add to her company's portfolio.

"Don't you think we need more designers now that the company is growing?" a head designer suggested during their meeting, others backing up the suggestion as a good idea.

"I guess we have to scout for more talents then," she added, agreeing with them.

She had over thirty staff working with her permanently, and more were still needed. They also needed the bigger space she had just acquired. It was the first office they'd need to do little or no renovations.

Presently, Flair and Design was worth approximately over a hundred million naira, generating more in revenue. They had made a name for themselves in the industry and had even grabbed the attention of the outside market, outdoing themselves.

Fifteen years ago, she dreamt of owning her own architectural firm, not knowing she would fall in love with interior design. She never worked under anyone when she graduated from school, even when her own parents doubted she would make something good out of herself by starting a business, but she ended up surprising them, uplifting their family name and reputation. She had co-founded Flair and Design with a male cofounder she graduated from university with, but he left after two years of founding because there wasn't any progress when they began.

He had packed his luggage and left the company to relocate to America where he believed he would make something out of himself. Later, hearing what Flair and Design had turned into afterwards he began to make trouble. Thankfully, before he left he had sold all his shares to her, making it impossible to win the lawsuit he filed against her. He was adamant and believed his sweat and blood made the company but she reminded him that he had left two years after foundation, everything that made Flair and Design what it was today was all because of her.

Mama Rere had called several times through the day but she chose to ignore them. She had also left voice messages via *WhatsApp*. And it wasn't because she was remorseful or anything, but because she was angry that her daughter disrespected her ever-able reverend who was nothing but a complete whore according to her. Thankfully, Ijeoma called at her usual time, typically when she was driving home from work and they talked through the trip.

"Babes, your mother is something else," Ijeoma commented when she heard the full gist.

She could not agree more. She could now see her mother's obsessiveness - it had gone beyond an African mother syndrome.

"But we shouldn't blame her. I'm sure she's just concerned about you," Ijeoma assured her.

The word 'concerned' turned her off. "Am I a child? She just treats me as if I'm one, and it's annoying."

"You're her only child, I'm sure she wants the best for you."

The best wasn't what Mama Rere wanted from her but to be normal like the rest of her peers. *Normal* job. A *normal* life with a husband. *Normal* children that took after her, but because she was abnormal, she had become a curse.

"So if you had agreed, that man was ready to commit adultery?"

"You should have seen how ready he was when he came to my house. I should have known better, judging by the eyes he used to give me during church services. What a pervert! I'm sure his wife has no idea and I can't wait to tell her."

"Maybe you shouldn't," Ijeoma advised.

"Why?" she didn't see any reason not to, after all, it was the right thing to do.

"Don't you think she may also get hurt in the process? You know how vulnerable these pastor's wives are, always getting blamed for their husband's shenanigans."

Ijeoma was right to believe so. It would have been cruel of her to report back to his wife after all the woman might even be in the position that she can't defend herself. They went on to discuss the sperm donation, and she happily reported to have found a willing donor.

"What about Folarin? You don't want to give him another chance?"

"Folarin? I don't know where he is. All I know is that he had left Nigeria," she scoffed.

"Don't tell me he left without saying a word to you?"

She did not have to say a word, Ijeoma already knew the obvious.

"What is his problem? What does he really want from you?"

"I don't even want to think about him or anything, I just want to focus on getting pregnant," she said sharply.

"I hope he won't return again with his nonsense. Goodbye to bad rubbish. I hope he reaps the fruit of his labour in the end," Ijeoma lamented, "I support you regardless."

"I know. Wish me luck."

"You don't need luck. You've got this."

16

Folake visited her gynaecologist with Akeem. Everything needed to be signed had been attested and sealed in the presence of a legal luminary. Before the visit to the hospital, she had to enlighten him more even though she had before, because he wasn't clear on what he was needed for. All he knew before was that they would need his sperm to fertilize her egg, and his thinking was that he would have to get her pregnant *manually*.

"I'm not going to sleep with you," she corrected quickly. Even though she'd considered it last night. He was far from her type: young. "We have to visit the hospital first and get you tested to know if you're the right candidate."

Akeem didn't seem convinced. Thankfully, her doctor was patient enough to explain things on the ground relating to the option she chose. IVF won't be as easy as they may have thought. The man had little job to perform, but she had to prepare her body with multiple injections to enhance her hormones before they could successfully transplant the embryo in her, and then she could get pregnant. So money wasn't everything when it came to having a baby the medical way, but her determination made her convinced that it was the right way for her.

"Doctor, is IVF that demanding?" she asked again just to know what she was embarking on.

"Actually, it is. You must eat a healthy diet, start taking prenatal vitamins, maintain a healthy weight, and also stop smoking or drinking alcohol," she strictly warned. "Thankfully, it won't stop you from doing your regular job!"

It was now left for her to adhere to all the warnings, especially the drinking part.

"What about him? What should he be careful of?" she asked.

"Just the same. His test results show he is capable, and by God's grace you will get pregnant!"

She was relieved to know Akeem turned out right,

that could have meant another recruitment drive if he wasn't.

"You must make sure to take two shots every day to enhance your egg growth until harvest."

The doctor had prescribed a hormonal injection called FSH, which will increase the number of her eggs until harvest time. Folake had made sure to pay all the expenses in advance. Her quest for a baby was very expensive, but she had more to spare in exchange for her joy and a chance to experience motherhood.

Optimistic about getting pregnant, she started injecting herself as the doctor instructed. She had also paid a sum of two million naira into Akeem's account, although he had rejected the offer as she had done more for her in the past, but paying the money was an assurance that it wouldn't be a problem in the future.

She called Akeem every day to make sure he was eating right and exercising as the doctor suggested. He wasn't supposed to engage in any sexual activity until they harvested his sperm, and he had sworn he had no girlfriend and wasn't frivolous. Her fear was him catching a sexually transmitted disease, but he had surprised her with not having a girlfriend.

"How's your mother recovering?" she asked abruptly, realizing she had never asked him and would usually forget to ask.

"She's doing much better, thanks to you," Akeem replied. "She has been disturbing me about wanting to see you. She wanted to thank you personally for saving her life.”

“I’m glad she’s doing fine. But...” She eyed him suspiciously as she continued, “I hope you haven’t told anyone about our deal?”

“Of course not. Why would I?”

“Not even to a family member, Akeem. Your silence and cooperation matter the most to me,” she said, almost pleading.

“Ma, I know what I’m getting into, and I will never tell a soul about you,” Akeem said in a tone she’d never heard him use. He got up to leave but retracted his steps. “I’m not someone that breaks an agreement, so you can rest assured that I won’t tell a soul.”

She watched him walk out dejected. She had hurt him with her words, and it wasn’t her plan to make him feel inferior. She only wanted a professional, straightforward relationship with him, nothing intimate.

She didn’t miss a day of her hormonal shots for the retrieval of her eggs. She had to brace herself to take the injections twice a day for the course of two weeks.

In the weeks that followed, her breasts became tender, her headaches increased, and she had serious mood swings. Coupled with that, she developed an insatiable appetite for food, which, as a result, made her feel bloated. She didn’t like the fact that she was adding weight, especially around her stomach, but she was trusting the process. Her period had ceased from coming, and her doctor had told her it was a sign that her eggs were getting ready for retrieval. Thankfully, she wasn't allergic to any of the shots she was taking as the doctor was more concerned she could face some complications.

Apart from the three who knew of her IVF journey, she didn't plan on telling anybody else until her delivery, not even her own mother.

She wished she could confide in her mother, but God knows what Mama Rere would say if she heard about the IVF journey. She had promised to give her a grandchild or get pregnant before the year ran to an end and before she reached forty, and now she believed it was Mama Rere's turn to wait.

She knew Mama Rere would judge her lifestyle, so it was better she kept things to herself.

She hadn't been taking her mother's call so she could be free emotional stress.

17

Folake visited the hospital a couple of weeks later to see how things were progressing. An ultrasound was performed to monitor her ovaries, and she had even done some blood tests just in case.

"I can see your eggs are increasing. You've been doing a good job so far," the doctor said.

Even though she was busy, she still found the time to comply with the doctor's instructions, thus yielding good results. She was also prescribed another hormonal injection called hCG, which will help in the maturity of her eggs till their removal. They had her booked for the following weekend, and she was advised to bring Akeem for his own extraction.

"Make sure not to eat or drink after midnight of the night of your retrieval. Most importantly don't use any scented lotions, hair products, not even makeup or perfume on that day," her doctor said solemnly. "Odours can be toxic to embryos."

She typed the information into her phone just in case she got carried away and forgot the most important things. She was the type to always spray perfume and put on makeup before leaving the house, and she could forget her doctor's warning about not performing her daily rituals, which would bring nothing but calamity, as her doctor had warned.

She had adhered strictly to the doctor's advise before coming to the hospital.

She was the one who drove Akeem to the hospital, having picked him up from his newly rented apartment; he made it a point to tell her that it was from the money she gave to him.

There, she lay on the hospital bed, sedated to sleep while a medical aide began the retrieval process, wondering about raising a child by herself. Knowing Akeem was in the other room while she was being sedated made her feel less alone.

When she woke up, she found she was being administered a drip to alleviate her nausea — the egg retrieval was a success.

"I didn't know which one you would like, so I got you

many," Akeem said soon after he handed her a black nylon filled with different kinds of biscuits and sweets.

She frowned in confusion.

"The doctor said you will need some sugar," Akeem said with an awkward smile.

"Thanks," she said. She was moved by his gesture that she unwrapped one of the biscuit packet. The doctor joined them a few minutes later.

"Your eggs and your sperm have been successfully extracted and taken to the laboratory for the next stage. You will be hearing from me as the process continues. But I'll advise you to take a lot of rest today. You will also experience some abdominal cramping, but it will be fine."

"Doctor, can I get discharged now?" she asked, glancing at her wristwatch. She was hoping to rest in her own house.

"You have to finish your drip first, in about two hours, you will be free to get discharged," the doctor said with a frown.

She was worried she might be keeping Akeem from leaving so she insisted she wouldn't need him anymore.

"You can't drive yourself home, Miss Awolowo. Let him be the driver for today," the doctor admonished.

Akeem volunteered to look after her throughout the day and he was doing his best to assist her at her vulnerable stage but she was concerned about being attached to him. Before leaving the hospital, she received a prescription for pain relief and was asked to avoid any strenuous activity for a day or two. Thankfully, it was the weekend, and she would use Sunday to rest.

"Make sure someone else administers the injection for you as it will be difficult to give yourself," the doctor said.

The only person close to her would be none other than Emma. Upon reaching home, she called her to ask for a favour in assisting her with the injection. Unfortunately, Emma was out of town with her own family. She didn't have anyone else to call upon and wouldn't want to involve Bimpe or any other person in her business, but she ended up inviting Akeem over to her house that evening to help her with it.

The injection was very painful and she was now regretting taking these extra measures to have a child of her own. It would have been better to have someone else to sleep with rather than endure this much pain. In her weakened state, Akeem was still there by her side through the night.

He could have gone to his own house after helping her with the injections but had stayed because she may have needed some form of assistance. She was in her room resting, bearing the pain even after taking some painkillers and was craving for something to eat. Her cook had travelled out of town and wouldn't want to bother Bimpe, so she asked Akeem to warm some leftover food in the fridge for her to eat. Only for Akeem to return with freshly made pepper soup and rice. He wanted her to eat some freshly made meal, and she was overly grateful he had stayed to look after her.

She devoured the food, and the nausea subsided.

Akeem watched her eat in silence.

While the rest were fast asleep in their rooms, she found him dozing off on the chair beside her bed when she woke up to drink some water. She watched him with awe. No one had ever been this kind and attentive to her before.

18

Folake's Sunday started in good spirits; the pain had subsided, and she could start her day without anyone's help, but she woke up very hungry. Akeem had slept over at her place, leaving Bimpe and the rest wondering about his identity and who he was to Folake. Bimpe had stylishly questioned him, and she told her he was nobody to her, only that he looked after her because of her little sickness.

"I didn't know you were sick," Bimpe said while they were in the kitchen preparing breakfast since her cook was yet to return from her trip.

"Just a little stress from work, and he has been so helpful to me," she replied, concealing the truth from her. She could have confided in Bimpe, and she could have been helpful in a way to her, but she feared that everyone might know about her business and that they might mock her for it. 'Just imagine a woman making a baby on her own', she knew they would say such things behind her back.

"Well, he's good-looking. I first thought he was your boyfriend," Bimpe added. "I wouldn't have believed he wasn't your boyfriend if he wasn't so young."

It would be a lie that she wasn't aware of his striking good looks; now, she had started noticing his good manners. Deep down in her heart, she hoped her future baby might take after his good looks and kind heart.

"Don't you think he's way too young to be a boyfriend?"

"Not at all. I think he likes you in some way," Bimpe assumed, but she wasn't flattered at all.

"Don't let your assumption get you into trouble, Miss Woman," she replied, dissuading the thought.

"I'm pretty sure my assumption is real," Bimpe defended. They were almost finished cooking when Akeem entered the kitchen, eager to help, but she told him to wait in the dining room and have breakfast with them before leaving.

"See, I told you," Bimpe whispered once Akeem left

the kitchen.

She shook her head in disbelief. She was the only person who knew why he was being nice to her, and it wouldn't be because he liked her. What was there to even like about her?

"I think you're only trying to sell yourself short. You're way more beautiful than you imagine," Bimpe said.

She didn't believe Bimpe. She never saw herself as the prize, men never rushed after her, and she never received any compliments about being beautiful while growing up. Mama Rere had even shamed her for not taking after her beauty.

"Just wait and see how things will turn around. I can attest to the fact that he secretly fancies you," Bimpe said.

She scoffed. She wasn't amused, not even optimistic about any future Bimpe had seen. She knew her type of man, and even though she looked the way she looked, she would never settle for less. Less meaning younger than her, she had always enjoyed the company of her age mates, never dreamt of becoming a sugar mummy to any younger man. Bimpe's last son, a boy of five years old, stormed into the kitchen demanding his food as he was very hungry and had become crankier. They hurriedly finished their cooking, served everyone their portions, and gathered around the big dining table, enjoying egg and yam.

Before Akeem left, he helped her administer the

injection. It was said she could take it any time, but it was better she did it in the morning before he left. She never bothered to check on work afterwards, instead, she took a long nap and ended up waking in the evening when dinner was made ready by her cook who had returned in the afternoon.

Her doctor called the following day to give a detailed report on the procedure. Ten of her matured eggs were retrieved and seven of them had been fertilized. "We're waiting for your fertilized egg to become an embryo, and it will take some days more."

A sense of relief washed over Folake as she received the news.

"Do you know that three or four of them might develop to the blastocyst stage," the doctor murmured excitedly.

"Does that mean I could get pregnant with twins?" she asked curiously.

"It is possible. We've had many women conceiving multiple births through IVF. Do you still want to keep the remaining eggs for future use?"

She hadn't thought of the future because she was hopeful about the present one.

"That's fine. We will be expecting you this weekend for the transfer," the doctor said before hanging up.

She screamed excitedly.

"I'm going to be a mother!" she kept repeating to

herself while she got ready for her day. She had yet to dress for work, and her day couldn't have been happier after hearing the news.

She would take a moment to caress her tummy, dreaming about the little thing that would grow inside of her. She wished for a girl child, a version of herself that she would give everything to. She dreamt of a happier and safer place for her upcoming child and wished to impact the knowledge she never had while growing up in the child.

"What if she grows up to become a lawyer?" she asked dreamily when Emma walked into her office.

"Aren't you the dreamer? But I can assure you that your baby will turn out right since she has a great mom like you," Emma replied, also in the right spirit as her boss.

"That reminds me, I have something important to pass across to you," Emma said, sounding serious. "I met with Winifred on Sunday, and she told me about her pregnancy, which Femi is responsible for."

"What? I can't believe this. Not only are they having an affair, they're now expecting a baby?"

She was beyond flabbergasted by the news. Thankfully, Bimpe has applied for a divorce suit.

"She told me Femi had neglected her completely, blaming his wife for intervening in their romance. That girl has no shame whatsoever," Emma hissed.

"I don't understand her at all. A beautiful girl like her

is selling herself short to an irresponsible man like Femi." She shook her head and rubbed her chin and found some strands of her had stuck out of it again. "What does he have that she's drooling over? He doesn't even have a good character to begin with."

No one knew Femi as she did; when they were little, she had witnessed how self-centred and rude he was, but his mother had encouraged such an act, being the only boy out of five girls. His sisters were good and were close to her. Only Femi believed the whole world should bow down to him.

"She's only reaping what she sowed, and I hope she learns her lesson before it's too late," she concluded. She later resumed work, concentrating her effort on the airport project. In the afternoon she visited the site again with Emma, inspecting every little detail while pointing out some corrections.

Mama Rere was calling non-stop all day, bombarding her with all kinds of messages as she had refused to pick up her calls at work. Since she had banned her from coming over to her house, Mama Rere now saw her as a bad daughter who didn't give honour to the woman who gave birth to her. In her text, she mentioned how rude it was for her to chase the reverend away; she never ceased mentioning that pervert reverend.

While ignoring her constant calls, she almost didn't answer Bill Carson, who called to ask after her. He was delighted to have heard about her IVF journey and praised her for being a strong-hearted woman.

"I know you're going to be a great mother," Bill commended.

"I hope you're doing great?" she asked, concerned.

"I'm great. I just caught the flu. I've been down lately," Bill replied.

"Make sure to prioritize your health over anything else. I wish I was there to keep your company," she said, though she was suspicious because he sounded like someone struggling to breathe.

There was a short pause from his end.

"One last piece of advice I have for you is to live life right and make sure to discover who has your best interest at heart. I can promise you that the person right for you will find you even if you're a distance away."

She was amused. Bill Carson believed in true love and having soul mates. She wished she had the strength of his belief even a little bit, and she wouldn't have jinxed herself on her previous dates.

"Fola-"

"I will make sure to put that in mind, Mr Lover," she teased, laughing with him.

She listened to more anecdotes before she bade him goodbye and ended the call. She wasn't on the path of finding true love that never existed for her, but what was in stock for her was raising a child of her own, and she couldn't wait for it to come true.

Throughout the week, Akeem would check in on her. He wasn't supposed to be that invasive in her life, but she strangely welcomed his concern for her. He wasn't even interested in her baby fever or whether what they did on the weekend was successful, only that he showed much empathy and sympathy about her wellness.

"I hope you're doing much better now, ma," Akeem asked, taking her by surprise. She was stunned by his good nature and saw him as someone who was generally nice to others.

"I'm doing great. Thanks for asking," she replied, feeling grateful for his concern.

"Just put your concentration on work," she cut in when he encouraged her to always call him whenever she needed help. She wanted to tell him Emma was doing that but asked almost eagerly, "I hope you're settling in just fine?"

She knew it was a ridiculous question as she had observed his progress since Femi left.

"Everything is going well, all thanks to you, ma," Akeem replied cheerfully.

She inhaled sharply when he smiled and almost choked. She stretched her hand to the glass of water which had been discarded the day before and quickly gulped it. She groaned in her mind. If he kept stopping by the office, he would make her wish to make her fantasies of him real and that would be a disaster due to their age difference.

"Do I get you more water?" Akeem asked.

"Mmm?" she answered distractedly.

"Water, more?"

She shook her head and gestured for him to leave.

As soon as Akeem left, she sighed, "This boy is going to get me into trouble."

19

On the day of her transfer, Emma was the one who drove Folake to the hospital. She wanted to make up for the last time by being present and helpful to her in her time of need. While Folake lay on the examination table after being given a medication that would help her relax, her doctor carefully inserted a catheter to open her up.

She felt the uneasiness as the tiny tube passed through her vagina, but it was something she had to bear. One could tell how excited she was, holding onto Emma's hand while the doctor diligently pushed the embryo inside of her. From the ultrasound, they all monitored the activity, which only took fifteen minutes, and it was a success.

"You will still experience some cramping or a little pressure in your belly, but I promise you that you will be fine," the doctor said, beaming with smiles. Folake was encouraged to still be taking some *Tylenol* to alleviate her cramps and take constant rest.

"Please avoid stress and any strenuous activity for some days. We will be able to test for pregnancy after a week or two. Fingers crossed," said the doctor before leaving the room.

She was moved to tears as she caressed her belly, dreaming about her future and couldn't wait to hear the news of her pregnancy. Emma was also moved to the point that she shed tears, praising her boss's effort and struggle.

"If you cry now, you're going to make me cry too," she said, playfully scolding Emma.

"How can I not cry? You're so brave!" Emma replied in tears. It was tears of joy, a moment Folake would remember for a long time and having someone to share it with was good enough for her. Folake was advised to stay for a while and rest, and when it was time to leave, Emma took her home. She did as she was instructed, relaxing on the bed and not working as she usually does. When she felt like not doing anything, she slept in and woke up late the following morning. Bimpe was worried she might still be down with a fever and went to check up on her, but Folake was now back on her feet.

"I thought you were still sick," Bimpe said when she entered Folake's room without proper knocking, which Folake didn't mind.

"I was only tired and needed some sleep," she replied. Although she was close to divulging her secret to Bimpe due to her happy mood, she held it in as she wanted everything to fall into place before announcing such news. Folake discussed Bimpe's job situation and also questioned about the ongoing divorce, which was going great, but wouldn't want to mention Winifred being pregnant with Femi's child. She thought it might hurt her if she heard about Winifred's pregnancy, even though she was going through a divorce.

"I've spoken to my banker friend, and he said there's an opening in his bank. I would have loved for you to work for me, but this job will benefit you in many ways. You don't have to worry about anything. Just go and do the interview," she encouraged.

"Not many women would dare to assist me in this kind of situation," Bimpe said and added, "Even our mothers," and finished with a eulogy.

She stood by nodding. She was surprised she was not stopping Bimpe like she always did.

Throughout the week, Folake was conscious not to overdo things or take up many tasks at work. She had designated Emma to fill in for her, making constant stops at the site on her behalf while she focused on the palace rebuilding project. She was supposed to travel down to another state to meet with the palace aides but had to postpone her.

She was already scheduled for that weekend for the pregnancy testing. She was bloated, and her breasts hurt. But when she started seeing some spotting, she began to panic, thinking something bad was happening to her, afraid of risking a miscarriage without being confirmed to be pregnant.

"It's normal to experience some spotting, but if it becomes a heavy flow, do come to the hospital immediately," the doctor urged.

She was slightly relieved upon hearing the news, but she wasn't able to take her mind off the spotting every time she saw it. Her anxiety sprung up like a fireball, thinking it might get worse or wake up one morning heavily covered in her own blood.

She was worried through her drive to the hospital to receive confirmation from her doctor. Her heart was beating sporadically like it was being pounded, her feet were shaking, and so was her hand. She jittered on the seat, waiting for her doctor to enter the office with her result, and was wondering if the result was going to be a positive one or negative.

"Congratulations, Miss Folake, you're indeed pregnant," said the doctor as soon as she entered. She walked in with a smile, and Folake knew what the result would be judging by the doctor's expression without having to say it. Folake had her mouth covered in joy, overwhelmed and happy that everything turned out right in the end.

"Doctor, so I'm going be a mother?"

"You already are. Congratulations once again," the doctor said, smiling.

She felt like screaming and shouting it to the world but was only keeping her cool so as not to alarm her baby.

"You finally arrived," she said softly, caressing her stomach. In the heat of things, tears trickled down her cheeks. She didn't even know why she was crying. She never thought she would know the feeling of being a mother, and of course, it wasn't her first time, only that this time, she was in control of keeping what was hers.

"I will still want you to take much rest, and please eat well. In about a week or more you will start to experience some severe morning sickness, but I can assure you that you will be fine."

"Doctor, will the bleeding still continue?" she asked worriedly.

"Like I've said, it's normal to see some spotting at this early stage, you should only be alert when it's heavy. Please, and please, don't stress yourself. This period should be about yourself, not work."

"I understand."

As soon as she arrived home, she called Ijeoma to tell her the ever-awaiting news, but she could only whisper as there were people in the house. Ijeoma was also moved to tears, happy to know her dear friend was pregnant at last.

"I'm going to be an aunty," Ijeoma screamed happily, almost breaking her eardrum.

"Have you told your Mom? I'm sure she will be praising the highest God by now."

"No, I haven't, and I don't plan on telling her now."

"Why not?" Ijeoma abruptly questioned.

"Have you forgotten what she did to me? Bringing that reverend to my house." She would also want her mother to share the joy of the news, but her worries were that her mother was a rattle-teller and she might tell the world about her pregnancy and people could start talking.

"I don't want that publicity on my head or my baby's."

She lay on the bed, carefully caressing her belly.

"I like the sound of that already. My baby!" Ijeoma cheered.

At this point, she was ready to give everything up for that child. She felt fortunate to have made the decision to have a baby at this age when it was slightly possible to become pregnant. Her world was now adding up. She was thinking of a nearby kindergarten where she would send her baby girl off and choose her outfits to match hers. She could send her abroad for her secondary education and for her tertiary education; she had the money anyway.

"Are you going to have the baby in Nigeria?"

"Actually, I've been planning to give birth in the UK. I just hope to have finished the airport project by then."

Even if she wasn't finished by then, she was thinking of handing the project over to her team since they would have been halfway done or almost finished before then. Her joy doubled when she received an email confirming her as one of the women in Africa to be selected for the entrepreneurship awards that year. Not only would she be receiving an award but was also selected to grace the cover of the African Forbes magazine as the next woman in business.

"Ma, I think this year is made for you. Everything is just turning out right!"

Emma jubilated with her. All her employees had also congratulated her on the victory and were indeed happy as their company would be thrown into the limelight after many years of hard work. Folake was blasted with all kinds of praises left and right, even from people who hardly spoke to her, but upon reading about her achievement, they called her phone to jubilate with her.

Her father also called during work hours to offer his congratulations. It was awkward for the two as they hardly communicated. Her father was unlike her mother, who would forever be included in her life regardless of the situation. Her father didn't have the courage to maintain a relationship with his own daughter.

Or maybe she was the one pushing him away since she had lost respect for him when he started going out with multiple women, abandoning Mama Rere, who was deprived of his love and attention. Most importantly, she was terrified of him; they could have easily amended their relationship now that she was older, but deep down she had yet to outgrow her trauma.

"I'm proud of you," he said on the phone, his voice sounding terrified and awkward, and so was her own.

"Thank you, sir," she replied. They didn't bother asking about each other's wellness; she already knew he was doing fine; after all, he had a woman who gave him everything he ever needed in life. She didn't bother to ask about Mama Rere; even in her time of celebration, she still chose to ignore her.

She wanted to call Emma but was distracted by the doorbell. Not long after, she heard someone running up the stairs, and in her concern, she got up to get the door when Emma barged in.

"What did the doctor say?" Emma asked.

She blinked in confusion.

"What did the doctor say?"

"Oh," she said with a snorty laugh. "I'm pregnant."

She watched Emma jump several times in her heeled

court shoes and knew she wouldn't be wearing them for some time. Then Emma stopped abruptly and began to rummage through her bag.

"I have a list of names for the baby and –"

"Emma, where are your manners?"

"At home. I stole my husband's car because he won't bring me over."

She blinked back tears. She didn't have to celebrate alone.

She sat beside Emma, and they were quiet for a long while.

"I think we should hold a party to celebrate you," Emma suggested to her while they were on-site to check the progress of things a couple of days later.

"Party?" She found the idea of the party to be an extravaganza.

"Yes, for the baby and for international recognition."

"I would love that, but I say we celebrate after collecting the award. Don't let us be overjoyful."

She was hoarding the fear of people sabotaging her or attacking her joy. She grew up with the fear instilled by her own mother that there are some village people who wouldn't like her success, so therefore she must keep to herself.

"Champagne would have been nice," Emma teased, still in the mood to hold a celebration. After all, they deserved it.

"In that case, everyone will receive their bonuses this week."

Emma screamed for joy, tightly hugging her.

She gawked at her assistant.

"Of course, there's nothing more important than money itself."

"I'm thinking of sending a lucky employee on a vacation to Seychelles, all expenses paid by me," she added.

"I pray to be selected for that trip, I need some vacation away from my little minions."

"I thought you couldn't do without them?"

"When there's a free vacation involved, I'm sure their father can manage them by himself," Emma replied, desperate enough to volunteer herself to enjoy some alone time away from her children.

She exhaled deeply and they began to their back to the Lagos traffic.

20

Folake fell ill during the second week of her pregnancy. She was down with her morning sickness and had to send her abled trusted co-designer on the trip she could have gone herself. She had tendered her apology to the King himself for not being able to show her face but entrusted her employee to take clues of things needed for the project.

Her once-growing appetite had disappeared, and she now hated the smell of some particular food. She would doze off on most occasions, her agile body that was always eager to work had become lazy and tired. She had developed some crazy cravings for things that were odd, like the smell of petrol and soap.

She was infuriated by the smell of her favourite perfumes and loathed anyone who passed her by reeking of one. Bimpe had become suspicious of her now that she started showing these symptoms, and had even diagnosed her before she could confess she was pregnant with a child.

"Aunty Folake, that's good news. I'm still mad you keep it away from me, but I'm happy you're finally becoming a mother," Bimpe congratulated. But Folake pleaded with her to keep the news to herself as she wouldn't want her mother to know just yet, or anyone in particular.

"I totally understand you," Bimpe assured. "Is he the one responsible?" She questioned, implying Akeem to be responsible for it.

"Yes, somehow. I used his sperm in an artificial way."

"Have you told him about the pregnancy?"

"No!"

Until now she realised she was yet to share the news with Akeem. It wasn't a big deal and their relationship didn't extend to sharing such personal information, but because he was being nice to her, she thought it wouldn't be a bad idea to tell him. Only that he was out of the country after winning the employee's vacation benefit, which was rather lucky being on his side.

"And you don't want to have anything to do with

him?" Bimpe instigated.

"Why would I? He's very young, and his life is just starting."

"I still believe he has a thing for you, and it would be a great idea for you both to get together." Folake wouldn't want to welcome the idea Bimpe was putting in her head, there was no way Akeem would like his boss, not even the slightest opportunity would allow such. "I don't believe so. Can we talk about other things?"

"How's your divorce suit going? I hope you're filing for half of whatever he owns?" Seeing Bimpe reluctant to give an answer Folake started doubting if she was indeed serious about the divorce or was still being threatened by Femi.

"Bimpe, I hope he hasn't been filing your head with threats. You can ask for whatever you want from him, and he wouldn't dare not do it." She drew Bimpe closer, encouraging her to pursue whatever fear away. "Your lawyer will get you anything you seek from him, and I'm sure they will do a great job."

Bimpe let out an uncomfortable smile, she was indeed hiding something from Folake, but her conclusion was that the divorce wasn't the problem but her new job.

"I don't know how I'm going to survive this new job. You know it's been long since I worked, I'm afraid of being a disturbance to them."

"Come on, I know you to be tedious and accountable,

I'm sure you will get used to it in no time. Or should I tell your boss to ease things for you?"

"No, you don't have to!" Bimpe interjected, She smiled an awkward smile, denoting how uncomfortable she had suddenly become. "I'm sure I'll do well."

She still wondered if there was something else going on with Bimpe, but she didn't want to be intrusive since she appeared uncomfortable. She didn't even have the energy to be intruding on other people's business. Everything she ever asked for had been given to her, and she could only be grateful for it. Now that everything was going great for her, it was then Folarin decided to reply to her text. It had been over a month and he now saw the messages she sent out of desperation, but guess what? She had passed that stage of desperation and wouldn't be needing him anymore.

In his text, he apologized for not replying sooner, stating how much she must have missed him when he left. How cocky of him, she thought.

"Do you think my world revolves around you?" she said as she read his messages. She didn't pay much attention to his text, didn't bother to text back, and even blocked his number and hissed loudly. "Good riddance to bad rubbish."

A week afterwards, her morning sickness ceased a little, and she could now resume working. There were times she worked from home, and her employees began speculating if she was suffering from an ailment. She had managed to conceal her pregnant state from them but not from Akeem, who now knew his sperm had germinated seed in her. He did what everyone had done: he congratulated her on her double happiness.

"I hope you're taking good care of yourself?" he asked, amusing her with his curiosity about her wellness. She recalled what Bimpe had said about the possibility of him liking her, but she quickly dismissed the thought.

"Thank you for your kindness," she slurred and stiffened.

Haba! What is this again? Why do I have to feel funny whenever you're around?

She wanted him to leave, but couldn't find the right excuse. He was there to make a report, but she wouldn't care to listen to him, but that voice of his turned

her rational mind to desires.

"Folake, what's wrong with you?" she scolded herself, reprimanding her overdoing acts. "He's just a child, you idiot." She blamed Bimpe for putting ideas in her head, and now she couldn't stop thinking about such ridiculousness. She focused on her work to get her mind off such a possibility and even visited the airport site again with Emma.

Everything happening with the project was going according to plan, and she made sure she double-checked if they were using the right materials for the project. The last project she got taught her lessons not to rely on and fully trust some contractors. Because she had trusted they would use the materials she bought for them, they ended up opting out for cheaper materials unbeknownst to her, causing much damage to her company's reputation.

She was no longer spotting, but she suffered painful cramps; the doctor told her to cease walking long distances. It was sometimes mild and would vanish as soon as she rested her body, but once she rose to do some chores or drive herself to work, it would return, repeating the same cycle for a week. She had hired a personal chauffeur to drive her around but had to fire him as he was such a reckless driver. Folake wouldn't want anyone putting her life and, most especially, her unborn baby in danger, as she prioritized the baby's safety over hers. Whenever she needed someone to drive her home after a tired day from work, Akeem was there to offer a helping hand. She would, most of the time, sleep while he drove; she had become used to his driving and somehow trusted him with her life. As this continued, some of her employees were speculating whether they had something going on, but Akeem had debunked such rumours.

But things got heated when an article was published in the business column, speculating that she was the boss that used nepotism and favouritism. An insider had confessed that she employed one of her latest employees because of the personal relationship they shared, even revealing that she could be carrying his child. There was much detailed information revealed in the article which had now rendered her helpless as this was the kind of scandal she feared the most.

"Why now?" she fraught about in her office, biting her fingernails, and was unable to go downstairs to confront the sea of reporters swarming around their workplace. At that moment, Emma walked in with Akeem. She had asked for the two to show up in her office, and she screamed at them both, questioning if any of them sold her out.

"Ma, I didn't do anything. You should know by now that I can never betray you." Emma eyed Akeem, acting suspicious of him already, but he also confessed he wasn't the one.

"I promise you ma, I can never hurt you," he replied pitifully. She was shaking, she no longer had control of her own emotions. Forbes magazine had called her, relaying how disappointed they were after reading the article, she couldn't even defend herself, knowing that when they heard her own side of the story they would understand. Or would they not? She wasn't sure now.

"Who now knows something I only told the two of you?" she worriedly questioned herself, only to recall that she also told her best friends, Ijeoma and her in-law Bimpe. But Ijeoma was the last person to suspect since she wasn't even living in Nigeria.

"Oh my god! Could it be Bimpe?"

"But why? For what reason would she sell me out to the press? Oh...wait...Femi. He had to be the one."

Folake grabbed her car key and pushed Akeem, who was offering to drive her home, aside.

"Stay out of my business," she blasted, forging her way outside. She managed to navigate her way out of the crowded press who were screaming out their lungs, asking both relevant and irrelevant questions that she chose to ignore.

In full rage, she raced home, ignoring the fact that she was suffering an excruciating cramp. It felt like period pain, and she must have overstressed herself. While holding onto her belly, she drove with one hand. Her mind was fuzzy, and she could only think of the betrayal from Bimpe, but she still wasn't sure why she would tell anyone her secrets.

Mr Aleshinloye cautioned her to take things slow when she saw how worked up she was alighting from the car.

"Where's Bimpe?" she demanded.

Mr Aleshinloye led her inside, still trying to pacify her.

"Where is she?" she screamed. Her pain had become unbearable at this point, but she was managing to hold on. Bimpe rushed down the stairs.

"Aunty Folake, what happened?" Bimpe asked, looking worried.

"Did you tell anyone about my pregnancy? Did you

tell Femi about the pregnancy?"

"I...I" Bimpe stuttered.

"Did you tell him or not?" she asked sternly. She wasn't the type to get angry easily, but her career and company were now at risk, and she wouldn't forgive anyone who used it against her.

"I'm sorry I told Femi," Bimpe confessed.

"Why? For what reason would you tell that douchebag of a man my trusted secret?"

"I'm sorry, Aunty Folake, but I'm getting back with him," Bimpe said casually.

"What do you mean by you're getting back with him? Are you both not getting a divorce?"

"I'm no longer getting a divorce," Bimpe murmured, turning her body away from Folake.

She gawked at Bimpe in disbelief through the excruciating pain she was bearing. All her efforts to get freedom and peace for Bimpe were futile.

"Is he threatening you?" she asked softly, hoping it was Femi's threat because there was no way these could make sense.

"No, he's not. I can't give away my marriage because of a little situation we have."

"But he beats you and cheated on you. Why must you believe that he will change? Why must you forgive him?"

"He has apologized and told me we can work things out, and I can't let you decide my life for me, Aunty

Folake," Bimpe loudly declared.

Forgetting her pain briefly, she said, "Bimpe, you shouldn't do this to yourself. He's a manipulator and narcissist, and I know you're aware that he's gaslighting you. Did he mention that Winifred got pregnant for him?"

Bimpe hesitated to reply and then said cooly, "I have to be a good wife, Aunty Folake. You will be able to understand me if you have your own husband."

"Are you for real?"

Mr Aleshinloye hovered, his hands in a plea to the two women.

Bimpe casually walked out on her, leaving for her rooms upstairs, while she tagged along.

"Bimpe, I know he's feeding you lies, but you shouldn't be a fool for him anymore. This is your life, and I want you to make your own decisions."

"Aunty Folake, don't be a home wrecker. I know that you're jealous of me for being married, but I can't let you destroy my life because you've refused to bring a man home."

A pain coursed through her chest at Bimpe's harsh words. Tears trickled down her cheeks as she murmured, "It shouldn't have been you, Bimpe."

As Bimpe swung her hand in the air to break free from her grip, she fell down the stairs, rolling until she hit the ground. Mr Alenshinloye rushed to her rescue, and by the time Folake recovered from the shock and the fall, her dress was already soiled with her own blood. Not the blood coming from any wounded part of her body, but her private part.

"No, no, no, it can't be."

She shook her head in fear. Her hands vibrated in shock, and she was no longer herself as she gathered the blood with her own hands, trying to undo what had just happened.

Seeing what she had caused, Bimpe rushed to her side, remorseful.

21

"Mr Alenshinloye, it can't be. It can't be," Folake cried. She wished it was a short nightmare, something she could wake up from. Her eyes were sweating tears, and her body was shaking in fear, and the worst thing of it all was that she had lost the pregnancy. Her cook came out to witness the ordeal and she was shaking.

Everyone was sobbing, but Folake's voice was the loudest. Mr Aleshinloye rounded her up in a warm embrace, a comforting place that she was able to cry on. She did for some minutes, crying about her life, her failures, her dissatisfaction, and most importantly about the God-given gift that was departing.

"Madam, let's go to the hospital," Mr Aleshinloye whispered. As he assisted her up, but she would rather remain where she was, covered in her own blood.

"Everything will be fine. I'm sure the baby will be fine too," Mr Aleshinloye assured her.

"I think so too, Mr Aleshinloye. It's just a little blood, I'm sure the doctor will say the same thing," she agreed and finally let Mr Aleshinloye carried her to her car. He said calming words as he drove her to the hospital.

While she lay in the theatre room, she reflected on a similar but more morbid scene from her past - an abortion. How she laid on her back, the pain she endured, and how she felt after the procedure. Apart from the overbearing pain she withstood, there was something particular that changed about her that she couldn't tell anyone. For weeks she had cried and detested herself for killing a poor soul. She felt like a murderer and silently loathed herself for it, but she managed to survive. Only that this time she didn't know how she would survive this.

After the evacuation, she was sent to rest in a private room where she received all kinds of visitors including her mother who just heard about the pregnancy and her miscarriage, and she wasn't happy that her daughter had kept all these away from her.

"All of these wouldn't have happened if you'd told me about the pregnancy. Now see your life, and where it ended," Mama Rere rebuked.

Unmotivated to talk, argue, or even eat the food that was brought to her, she whispered, "Mommy, can you please leave me alone? I want to be all by myself."

When Mama Rere opened her mouth to speak again, she turned her back to her and covered her head.

"What is wrong with you, this child? You take everything for granted, and that is your problem. If you've allowed that reverend to do his job that day, I'm sure such evil would have been averted from your side, but look where you ended up."

She balled her hands and got up.

"Get out, Mommy. I don't want to see you or anybody."

When Mama Rere wouldn't leave, she pushed her out herself, shutting the door, and slid to the floor and cradled her chest to mourn for her baby.

"Why me? Why me?"

Mr Aleshinloye entered the room while she was striking her chest.

"It's going to be fine," he said, patting her back.

She kept repeating negative words to herself, but Mr Aleshinloye tried to make her stop.

"You don't understand, Mr Aleshinloye. I'm finished, and it's over for me."

"No, it's not over. You still have many chances to do

whatever you want. You're young and blessed. I'm sure the heavens will open their door for you soon," Mr Aleshinloye encouraged.

Before she was discharged from the hospital, Bimpe had left the house with her children. (It was Mr Aleshinloye who gave her advice to leave, not for Folake to meet her there; he believed it could cause her more harm if Bimpe was still there in the house with them.)

For days, Folake locked herself in her room. She was hardly eating, and avoiding work. All she did was sleep and drink. She had gone back to her old ways, drowning herself with more alcohol, and she wished she could end her own life. It was just a thought until it became something she hoped to manifest. The thought of suicide swept her mind; she could no longer see herself as the same Folake who was extinguished among her peers.

She was absentminded and barely acknowledged Mr Aleshinloye and her cook's efforts. Food was tasteless, but alcohol served her taste buds right, its bitterness and intoxicating aroma.

She switched off all her phones. It seemed to have scared her friends; even Akeem came begging to see her. Sleeping on the floor was comforting but made her fall sick. She had developed a cold and catarrh, which she didn't want to recover from it.

Emma was said to have dropped by while she was

avoiding everyone. She didn't want their comfort and words of advice because she felt she didn't deserve them. On occasion, she would have the same nightmares - seeing herself covered in her own blood, crying fervently while her baby desperately called to her. Along with these dreams, she started sleepwalking, waking up in absurd places.

Days turned into weeks, and she was still not out of it. Her cold was treated under the care of her doting cook who made sure she had some herbal concoction after eating, forcing it down her throat as she would scream and reject being fed.

While she shunned everyone, her two favourite people living with her bore her pain, sympathised with her, and cared for her, and it was only when she started getting better that she realized what they had done for her. She had now reduced her alcohol intake and was now sleeping comfortably in her own bed, but there were times she would sleepwalk.

She was still hesitant about having guests over or receiving their calls. She just wanted her alone time and didn't want to be bothered with work just yet. In her time of depression, the person she would want to see last was whom she ended up welcoming with her whole heart. Folarin had just returned from America, heard what had happened to her, and decided to pay her a visit.

Folarin was the only person who had access to her. It was more like she wanted him closer just to punish herself. This was the same man that left without speaking a word to her, wasn't there in time of her need, but now he suddenly appeared out of the blue once again. He was kind enough to also look after her, asked how she was fairing as days went by, and she had become used to his company.

She had invited him into her room, and both would spend alone time in her room. She was getting cosier in his embrace. He started kissing her on the cheeks; then it proceeded to them making out for minutes. She was clearly not herself those times; she wasn't putting herself first, and she knew she was punishing herself, thinking it might help her heal.

She demanded sex from him to make her feel better, but instead of feeling better afterwards, she just felt worse. His touches weren't the same as she knew it to be, even his kissing techniques were somehow. Sex with him had become boring, or maybe she was the one that had become boring. She would pretend to enjoy his performance.

"Can we just stay like this all day?" she demanded, but when she stopped faking her satisfaction, they stopped having sex.

"If that will make you feel better," he said to her, snuggling her tightly and not letting her slip from his embrace. They also discussed other things, like his ongoing divorce, and he apologized for leaving her without telling her what happened.

"I had to sort out some family crisis, and you wouldn't believe I got my phone confiscated by my children's mother. She thought she could use her superiority over me."

"How about now?" She gazed intently into his eyes, wanting to know his present predicament and position, thinking she could offer her help to him in a way that would make him feel better.

Folarin coughed, smiled and kissed her hand. "She has become my ex now. We've parted ways."

She would want to talk about the past, what took place in his absence, and how she almost had his child, but she didn't have the confidence to bring it up. Not now, she convincingly said to herself whenever such a thought crossed her mind.

"When will you get back to work?" Folarin asked.

She didn't know the answer to that, and she was not even sure she would want to resume work at the moment. She was one hundred percent sure that her team was working hard in her absence, doing a fantastic job on her behalf. She trusted Emma to fill in for her, making rounds at the site to check the process of things. If there was an emergency, she would know.

"Honestly, I don't feel like working. My body feels like a shutdown computer that can't reboot itself."

"I think you should try going for therapy. I heard it will help," Folarin suggested.

"Therapy? What? Do you think I'm mad?" she snapped.

"I don't mean it in a bad way. I just hope you can get some counselling regarding the way you're feeling. I also attended therapy with my wife... I mean my ex-wife in the past."

"How easy life must have been for you," she scoffed at him. Irritated and annoyed, she stood up and asked him to leave.

"I'm only looking out for you, Folake. You need to get your feelings and emotions checked, or else it will become a trauma for you," Folarin explained, resting his hands on her shoulder, but she shrugged it off.

"What do you know about trauma, Folarin? What do you even know about me?" she cried, sniffing and resisting the urge to bring up the past.

"Folake, I know you better than anyone else. You're this magical living being that touches people's lives and cares for them more than you even care for yourself."

"So you know that, and you still used it against me?" she asked.

"No, I did not," Folarin replied.

"Yes, you did, Folarin. You did twenty years ago. Do you even know what took place in your absence?" She took a deep breath, finding her momentum. "Why didn't you tell me you wanted to leave for America? Was I not important to you? Was I some chop-and-clean mouth?"

Folarin looked confused for a bit and walked towards her. "Folake, you were my first love, and I know you know that I loved you."

"You don't lie to someone you love. You don't keep things from them, and worst of all, you don't abandon them in time of their needs." She wiped the tears trickling down her cheeks.

"I'm sorry, Folake. But I thought we've passed that stage already. We are cool, are we not?"

She didn't like the fact that he took her feelings for granted. She believed he could at least try his best to ask for forgiveness. Maybe she could have been healed from the past if he did, not assuming things were fine between them because she said so.

"Can't you at least pretend you care for me? Even if it's for once."

"Folake, I don't have to pretend when, in fact, I care for you. If I'm not after your health, do you think I'll be here supporting you?"

Folake was exhausted at this point. There was a point in trying to get some empathy out of him when he clearly didn't have one for her to begin with. She had been the biggest fool, chasing after him and loving him, but he just received those feelings like his birthright and never thought of reciprocating them.

"Just leave, Folarin. You've done enough for me, and I think we should end things here," she sighed, relieved. She had decided.

"I will leave for now because you want me to, but I promise to be back. We are not done, Folake. You've to tell me everything I did wrong to deserve this kind of treatment from you."

She shook her head but let her tears flow.

22

Folake's working spirit returned to her after her last encounter with Folarin. He, who promised to return after their last argument, has yet to show his face or call her. She didn't even want to be bothered by his impromptu appearances anymore. Since he saw her as someone who needed therapy before regaining her life back, she wanted to show him and the world that she wasn't crazy, and what better option than to start going to work?

Her sudden appearance in the office was a shock and a relief to her employees who had missed her leadership and guardianship. Although she wasn't as optimistic or enthusiastic as the rest, she just wanted to get by her days. She acted unbothered when Emma asked how she had been the whole time.

"My world is not crumbling down, Emma. Let's get back to work," she replied firmly. Her old Folake was yet to return, but she still managed to run the company like she used to. The airport project was halfway through under Emma's leadership, and she had taken it from there when she resumed. Forbes magazine had also called and even sent a representative after their investigation, but she dismissed their concern and blamed them for doubting her in the past.

"Ma, don't you want to give an interview? They apologize for everything they said to you that day."

"Emma, I don't need anyone's sympathy anymore. It's too late for that now, and I certainly don't need their awards. They should give it to someone else," she angrily snapped.

Unlike before, she would have appreciated them apologizing to her and happily obliged to do their bidding.

"Ma, are you certainly all right?" Emma doubtingly questioned, she had been suspicious of the new Folake the whole time.

"Did I tell you otherwise," she snapped.

Emma quietly left.

Mama Rere came around in the evening; Mr Aleshinloye had invited her. Mama Rere was the last person she wanted to see apart from Folarin, but since she was there to settle some score with her she allowed her into her space.

"Maami, good evening. Welcome."

23

"Your bodyguard told me to come here," Mama Rere said sarcastically, acting like she didn't care enough to be there.

"What do you want, Mommy? I know you're not here because you cared about what anyone else told you."

"Why are you acting like this? Folake, all these happening to you happen to all women. You have to brace yourself and stop acting like a child that needs supervision."

"Mommy, what would you know about losing a child? What do you even know about me?" she asked in a tired voice. Instead of getting angry, she decided to find a reason why her Mother was always acting like an enemy. She genuinely wanted to know and was ready to squeeze some answers out of her.

"Mommy, most mothers I know would sacrifice anything for their daughters. I have never heard any of your friends being an enemy of their daughter's progress, but when it comes to you and me. It's never the case."

"If you have brought a man home, do you think I will be here screaming at you? I wouldn't even dare act this way in the presence of your husband, but because you have no man to defend you, I can always walk in here and talk to you because you deserve it. Folake, don't let my enemies laugh at your failure. You're almost forty. You should have been a mother to teenagers by now, not struggling to have a child of your own."

"But you told me to get pregnant by just anybody. I gave you what you asked for, Mommy," she cried, her voice rising.

"But where is it now? Haven't you lost it?"

Mama Rere's words pierced her heart, damaging her more than she had felt before. No one had said it with such boldness until now; hearing it from her own mother's mouth destroyed her completely.

"I told you to get pregnant by a man, but you went ahead to do it the *igbaloju* way. Are you trying to prove you're richer than every woman out there who doesn't need a man? I'm sure if you'd listened to me, this wouldn't have happened."

"Mommy, do you even love me?" she asked, her lips quivered as she spoke, and tears began forming in her eyes. "Did you ever love me?"

"Love is not what you need, Folake. You need the truth, and I'm the only one that can say it to you."

"And you don't ever think how *your truth…*" She air quoted. "Could hurt me?"

"That is the truth for you. It is meant to hurt you so you can do better." Mama Rere readjusted her *gele* proudly.

"So what do you want from me now?" she asked solemnly, feeling overpowered and defeated.

"Bring a man home or get pregnant. Why can't you be like those women who snatch men or become a second wife? But your pride wouldn't allow you since you're too big for it. What is the essence of having a big house, driving big cars, and being a company CEO when you don't have a man to call a husband? I'm a woman today because I married your father and had you. And I won't watch you not having the same."

She had accepted defeat; there was no need to convince Mama Rere that she was her own person, born with feelings.

"Ok, I'll bring a man home and get married like you want," she said, sniffing her tears in.

Mama Rere eventually left with a air of victory. Her mother had always held the keys to her unhappiness, and she couldn't even fight to be free.

Few minutes after her mother's departure, she was alerted of the presence of Bimpe, who came to apologize for her wrongdoings, but she would rather have her leave than welcome her into her home. All that happened to her was partly Bimpe's fault; if she had known, she would have kept the secret to herself or, better still, would not have welcomed her into her home. She could have listened to Mama Rere, who told her to mind her business; maybe she could not have lost the pregnancy.

"Please, she can tell you whatever she came here to say. I just need my sleep and peace," she urged Mr Aleshinloye.

"I believe she came to say sorry for what had happened," Mr Aleshinloye said.

"Tell her to return to her husband's house before he comes here to constitute a nuisance like he always does."

Mr Aleshinloye left. She overheard him relay her message to Bimpe.

"I can't sleep well at night, Mr Aleshinloye. It's all my fault that she lost the baby. Please let me talk to her."

"Em madam, that wasn't the only thing she lost. She lost a sister as well. I would never have thought you could betray her in such a way," Mr Aleshinloye admonished Bimpe. "Call her on the phone but give her time."

When she heard Mr Aleshinloye's words, she sniffed. If only her mother would defend just a little. She wondered what her life would have been like this past decade without Mr Aleshinloye and her cook.

She exhaled heavily, switched on one of her phones and went through her emails and contacts so that she realized how worried her close contacts were about her.

Ijeoma had called, leaving several messages after hearing the news from Mama Rere.

With a confidence boost from the conversation she'd overheard, she checked her email. There was an alarming email from a lawyer about Bill Carson's death—an invitation to the funeral proceeding that had taken place in her absence. There were several emails from Lord Anderson, Bill Carson's lawyer, telling her how urgent it was for her to show up for Bill Carson's last will and testament. While she was avoiding everyone, another misfortune had befallen her, and she had no idea of it until now.

She hurriedly packed a bag and a suitcase and made preparations for her travels. She wept through her trip and still couldn't control her tears when she landed at Heathrow Airport knowing he wouldn't be there to receive her like last time.

As she got out of the cab near Lord Anderson's office in Kensington, she was filled with a sense of loneliness and dread. It had been a week since Bill Carson's burial and he seemed relieved to see her.

"I was going through a life crisis myself, that's why I couldn't see the email sooner; I'm so sorry for what happened," she apologised deeply.

The old man smiled politely. "Please accept my condolences. He was a fighter, but the fight had been long."

She frowned. She heard a rumour that Bill Carson had prostate cancer years ago.

"Prostate cancer," she said. She recalled how weak he sounded in their last conversation. She blinked back tears and sighed.

"Bill Carson has always seen you as a daughter and had made you his next of kin. According to the law and the wording of this will, you're his sole inheritor. If you have time, we could go through his assets and some listings."

"Wait, what?" She gawked at the man's hair, wondering if Bill Carson still had his tight curls. "Heir?"

"He trusted you with everything after his death and would want you to continue being happy for him. He also left you a letter." The lawyer opened a drawer and handed her a folded envelope. "He told me wonderful things about you before his passing."

"And the will reads, I, Bill Carson, in my right mind and free will bestow upon Folake Awolowo…"

She gritted her teeth when he mentioned her name. She smiled; Bill was the first person who wasn't African to pronounce her name correctly. In everything, the lawyer said, she'd inherited the manor she'd stayed in on her last visit and fifty per cent of Star Holdings. She couldn't understand why Bill would leave her with such great fortune.

"You have a lot of paperwork to sign, and we have to prepare some documents for the share transfer in your name. I believe you will still be in town for a couple of days?"

"Yes, but I had scheduled my flight for next week because of work."

"That will do! Congratulations Miss Awolowo, and do accept my condolences."

They exchanged handshakes and contacts at the end of the meeting, and she left for the cemetery where Bill was buried. He was laid next to his wife, and now they could be together. She sat next to his, weeping for not being there sooner. She could feel his spirit present with her when she was there, he must have missed her as she was also missing him now. She brought his favourite flower, lilac, and placed it by his tombstone.

She returned to the hotel where she would be staying until she left to unpack herself and rest for the day. As she lay restless on the bed, she remembered the letter Bill had written and decided to read it.

Folake,

Don't be restless. Don't worry about the world. Don't worry about the future.

You're the star that has brought me hope and warmed my heart from the day we met at the conference, which was knocking my head for attending. I'm glad I reluctantly attended, or how could it be that I'd find a ray of sunshine?

Remember our last conversation and I remind you — it's okay not to have everything figured out. Believe in yourself and love yourself. Pursue happiness, okay? When love comes, you will know who that person is because you will feel it in your heart

I know with or without me, you'll do better.

I believe in you. Believe in yourself too.

And if you're ever in a messy situation, make sure to consult the people who truly love you.

Your mentor,
Bill Carson.

"You're the father I didn't know I had," she mumbled as tears poured down her cheeks. "If I ever find myself in a situation that is messy, I promise to consult the people who truly love me."

She wished she'd find someone she'd love enough to stay faithful to even after death the way he was to his wife. Bill had always insisted that she'd know true love if she came across it, because the person would be after her happiness, wouldn't judge her and understand her enough to want to be with her regardless of the situation.

She was overwhelmed with all kinds of emotions but trusted it was the best time to call Ijeoma whom she hadn't called in a while, taking Bill's advice. Ijeoma was as overwhelmed as she was losing a baby, sobbing together on the phone while unpacking a lot of things happening to them. She told Ijeoma about Bill's passing.

"Should I come to you?" Ijeoma asked.

"I'm in England oh! I had a meeting with Bill's lawyer this afternoon, he basically left me his properties."

"You don't mean it?" Ijeoma gasped.

"Oh yes, I don't even know what to feel about accepting all of these. He's basically the largest shareholder of Star Holdings, and now he's passing that to me. I get the part about household items but what do I know about shipbuilding?"

"Babes, I don't even know if I should be proud of you, or happy, or just keep quiet."

"I believe he would want me to be happy. But I'm not sure how to accept it as if it's birthright. I didn't even know he saw me like a daughter."

"That's life. You must have added value to his life. That's why I told you not to underrate yourself. People that will love you will love you, and they will make you feel special."

Ijeoma's words of comfort reinforced Bill's words.

She must put herself first, starting now, after all as the saying goes, a fool at forty is a fool forever. She would start a party. She decided to call Emma.

24

While Folake was on the flight back to Nigeria, news about her inheritance broke out. As soon as she saw Emma at the airport she knew something was up.

"What happened?" she asked calmly.

"You're trending o! I came to take you to my house because they've *paparatzeed* your house and the office complex.

Her phone rang, and she picked up without looking at the screen.

"The world knows, Babes. It's a midterm break, so I'll come with the kids."

"I don't think it will be safe for them. According to

Emma, my house has been *paparatzeed.*"

"Oh my goodness! Staying at a hotel would be worse," Ijeoma said with a whooshing sound.

"I'll hide at Emma's for some time."

She turned on her date and began to read the news. She was trending both online and offline as the heiress of the Star Holdings shares after the death of a prominent British business mogul. The news got leaked when the company did a press release honouring the decision of Bill's will, but they weren't supposed to expose her identity as it was against their protocol.

Blogs, social media, mainstream media, and newspapers across Nigeria wouldn't stop talking about the unusual bond between her and the deceased in the weeks that followed. Some speculated she was having an affair with Bill before his death; some said she only got lucky, and others just gossiped about her success and lifestyle and worse were the ones that claimed she had abandoned them in their time of need.

She knew she had to debunk some rumours as it was getting out of hand, especially with the airport project now under threat because some government officials were calling for her handover, but it was rather too late to hand the project over that she had spent a lot on.

"Contact Best magazine; I need to give an interview with them," she ordered Emma. Best Magazine was the only option she would go for as they had been there through thick and thin with them. She wouldn't acknowledge the rest who were eager to gossip about her since they didn't deserve to know her true story. Her once school mother from secondary school was the owner and founder of Best Magazine, and both women had shared a formal type of relationship that spanned over two decades. Hearing from her delighted Mrs Majek, and she made sure she oversaw the interview process and questions. She was also present when her brilliant interviewer started asking paramount questions relating to the scandals of the past and the present, and in the room with them was Emma and Akeem. Ijeoma had insisted it should be livestreamed.

"Folake Awolowo, you were selected among the women to bag the female entrepreneurial awards for this year, but somehow you got blacklisted because of a scandal that you slept with a male employee in order to give him a job?"

"I never slept with anyone," she replied sharply. She knew what was at stake and what the world wanted to know about her, and she was born ready for the interview to clear the air. "I'm a woman who's almost forty, never married and doesn't have any children. So you can imagine how the society views me as a woman."

She paused for a moment, swallowing her pride and wouldn't want to sound standoffish that would make people want to judge her lifestyle.

"I was dying to have my own offspring, so I made a

deal with a young vibrant gentleman who donated his sperm for me. I tried IVF and got pregnant, luckily, but sadly, I lost the baby."

As tears began to pool in her eyes, she noticed Akeem start to get up, but Emma put the folder she was holding in front of him and shook her head. She sighed with relief because she was certain if someone had given her a shoulder, she would have cried freely, so she dapped her eyes the way Emma had taught her a couple of minutes ago.

"I lost my baby," she repeated softly, trying her best not to sound hurt and dapped her eyes again.

"That's quite sad," the interviewer empathized. "I believe you're also aware of the present rumour of you having an uncanny relationship with the British Industrialist and Businessman. What do you have to say about that? It's quite uncommon for a woman like yourself to come of such fortune?"

"Are you implying I did something uncalled for just to inherit from him?" She sounded pissed off by the question.

Mrs Majek had to caution her employee, correcting her to sound professional and not go off script as planned.

"Bill Carson was more than a friend to me, he was like a father and mentor to me. You wouldn't believe that I was also shocked to have been called to hear his final words and will. And to the people out there who are disseminating untrue rumours about me and my company should get ready for a lawsuit, as I'm ready to take them up in court."

She wasn't joking about the lawsuit. Once her interview was published, it triggered another debate among her fans and anti-fans. Some, mostly females, fired at the people who were judging her lifestyle or mocking her for being unmarried at her age that she would need a younger man's sperm in order to make a child of her own.

Akeem was also picked on by his fellow men for being an opportunist who was paid off by a woman and was kept silenced. Even though he wasn't bothered by their claims, it became unbearable for him to show his face in public as his photos and address were leaked online.

She was confused at this point. She had thought the interview would suppress the rumours; instead, it had spiked another controversy. Her crisis management control team was also doing their best to control the damages done to the company. The head of the department had speculated that it only got worse as she was a female boss and that if she were otherwise, she could have gotten away with it.

"I didn't do anything to deserve this treatment. Make sure you do your job and make me victorious," she said.

They were just like her mother, they never saw anything good.

She remembered the words in Bill Carson's letter and sighed and chose to concentrate on people who truly loved her.

"Emma," she said as soon as Emma walked. "I want to throw an extravagant for my fortieth."

"Eh!?" Emma exclaimed, gawking at her.

25

When everything got dark for her, Lord Anderson came to the rescue; he was out of town when the rumour broke out. The lawyer pledged to sue Star Holdings for breaching the agreement between them and his client. His revelation managed to sway people over, and they no longer discussed how she came of the newly found wealth.

To think that it would take a man to make everything vanish reminded her that she was living in a man's world, the same world her mother had warned her about. She'd learnt from her cook that Mama Rere had fasted and went to several mountains on her behalf to pray she got out of the mess and found peace, most importantly, find a husband.

One of the trolls said that if she had just settled down and not pursued wealth, she wouldn't have remained unmarried at her age as if they knew her story, as if they were aware of all the downfalls and breakups in her life.

Alcohol began to taste sour taste in her mouth, and she remembered her resolve before travelling and the wordings of Bill Carson's letter and cleared her room of all forms of alcohol. Regardless of everything happening to her, she wouldn't want to get swallowed by it, and she had taken the advice of her gynaecologist, whom she visited recently to seek therapy.

"It's not your fault," her doctor encouraged. "It's sad to know that early miscarriages are very common amongst IVF carriers. But I'll encourage you to speak to a professional about the way you're feeling. It's not a stigma, and you shouldn't hate yourself for it."

The following week, she went to therapy. Having never attended, she was unsure of what to do or say, but she was beginning to think differently. She was raised to think everything happening to her was a result of her carelessness and lack of a prayer life, never having to take her mental health seriously. As awkward as it was for her to sit in an empty room with a stranger - a tall, slender woman extended her hand, and she didn't hesitate to reciprocate the gesture - she was meeting for the first time to discuss her life, it made her feel safe for some reason.

"Let's start with an introduction, shall we? I'm Titi, what's yours?"

"I'm Folake, and I'm new to therapy."

"Well done, Miss Folake. I must commend you for taking a bold step and coming to therapy today. I believe this is your decision?"

"Yes, Doctor Titi. I'm here because I believe I have a lot going on in my mind these days." She exhaled nervously, trying to maintain her calm and not to show how anxious she had been there.

"Take your time. There's no rush here. Do know that I'm here to help you reason out your feelings and better your mind." Doctor Titi smiled before taking out a journal and pen. "So, describe with one word how your life has been lately?"

She watched the woman eagerly pick up her pen and begin to write. It was her first time witnessing such a thing, and instantly felt like she was being interrogated.

"It's a safe space," Doctor Titi persuaded.

She took a minute to think. It was rather hard for her to put all her worries into one word, but she did come up with a resonating one.

"It's chaos."

Doctor Titi scribbled as she asked, "How chaotic?"

"Very chaotic. I just lost a pregnancy, was made a

villain in the news, my mentor recently died, and my mom..."

"I'm sorry for all of your loss," Doctor Titi said, her words comforted Folake and encouraged her.

"When I got pregnant through IVF, I thought I had hit the jackpot. Finally, my life would be complete, but all it took was one great fall, and down I rolled covered in my own blood." It had been hard recounting such a memory, but being in the presence of a professional, she managed to retell the unfortunate incident.

"Can you ever forgive the person that made you lose the pregnancy?"

"Could I?"

She wasn't sure.

"How did you cope through those times?"

"I drank to stupor, and I made love with the person that left a huge scar in my heart." She wasn't ashamed to talk about Folarin and what took place twenty years ago.

Doctor Titi stopped taking notes briefly.

"What made you want to punish yourself? Like you've said, your relationship with him ended twenty years ago."

"I thought it had until he showed up again, and I couldn't let go of him. Because I haven't told him about the pregnancy and the abortion." Her face fell when mentioning about her abortion; it was something she hated herself for.

"I have seen myself as a murderer after that abortion,

and I'm not even bold enough to confront my own mother on why she had forced it on me."

"You've mentioned your mother a couple of times. Could she also be part of what's causing you pain?"

She scoffed before answering, "Mama Rere knows how to make me unhappy rather than praise me. In her words, I'm nobody because I do not have a husband. And that it's my fault all these things are happening to me."

She didn't know when she started sobbing; it was an uncontrollable tear that took ten minutes before realizing she was in the presence of a stranger.

"I'm sorry."

"It's okay, this is a safe space," Doctor Titi urged, offered her a paper napkin and then waited for a while before saying, "I want you to do something for me as homework. Next session, I want you to bring a handwritten note about things you love about yourself. You don't have to think much; just write everything that comes to your mind."

As easy as the homework sounded, Folake was pensive to write all the things she loved about herself. She knew what she liked and didn't like about herself but had never thought of herself in a loving, intimate way. She grew up hating her own body as many of her peers were equally blessed with both buttocks and breasts, while she was flat-chested. She was equally insecure about her face and was never the centre of attraction.

She pondered in the bathroom, thinking of what to write. As Doctor Titi had said, anything could have easily popped into her mind, but it was rather a hard job to complete. She racked her brain trying to find answers, and it was only a day into her next session that she came up with some answers. She wrote about loving her kindness, her generosity towards others, and how independent she was, while Doctor Titi was nothing but amused.

"Intriguing. I was expecting something else, but this is quite fascinating."

She was now embarrassed of herself. "Did I do badly?"

"Not at all. There's no wrong or right answers. Only that your feelings reflect in your thoughts." As usual, Doctor Titi reached out for her journal and pen to jot down important talks.

"Don't you feel pretty? Many could have easily written about their appearance and cared less about what people say."

"Doctor, I don't look pretty, and it's fine."

"But if I tell you that you're beautiful, will you believe me?"

"I'll say thank you!" She smiled awkwardly.

She could recall the last someone called her pretty. It

had been Bill Carson. He sang her praises but she never believed it.

Doctor Titi fell silent, her eyes piercing through her reading glasses as she stared at the heavily guarded Folake. It was a fleeting moment of self-doubting for her, and she could tell she was a disappointment for not feeling beautiful enough.

"I would like you to take some minutes to convince yourself that you're beautiful. You can say it aloud if you want to." Doctor Titi said and left the room.

It was a hard one for her. Until now, she never realized how damaged she was, mostly to herself. How hard it was for her to think of herself as being beautiful and how hard it was to say those words.

"I look beautiful," she repeatedly said but wasn't convinced.

"You're beautiful!" she suddenly said, and in tears, she kept saying those words, and it was now coming true and easy for her.

"Folake, you're beautiful. You're beautiful, I'm beautiful," she had gone insane with it and wouldn't stop repeating those words.

Doctor Titi returned, meeting her in a state of self-admiration and joined her in the act.

"That's it, Ms Folake, you're indeed beautiful."

Since she started therapy, she'd been shedding constant tears and wasn't ashamed of it. Each time she cried, she felt relief. The doubt of not being good enough or beautiful was breaking away with spoken words of admiration and confessions; it felt like something heavy had left her chest, leaving her soul nourished.

26

Folake was now more confident and decided to take care of her body began early morning jogging. She preferred staying indoors to exercise so no one would judge her in the neighbourhood for being a single woman, but now she didn't care about the whispers.

In the weeks following her last session with the therapist, her make-up reduced, especially the need to conjure a longer nose. Emma had noticed. Her life was getting back on track, and all it had taken was a bold step to seek help and guidance. It gladdens her to have listened to her gynaecologist. Now, she was reaping the benefit of it and had gained the confidence she never had. She smiled often and didn't need any reason not to.

When Mama Rere called the other day, she didn't feel threatened; the leash her mother had on her was loose, although she still felt a little bothered by the noises of bringing a man home.

It was still dawn and it had rained overnight, but that didn't stop her daily exercise. It was quiet except for a few people who could be seen on the streets, either going to work or exercising like herself. Ever since she started jogging, she had come across quite a few men who would take glances at her whenever she passed by, but with her headphones in her ears, nothing else mattered. She was reaching her last lapse when she coincidentally bumped into Akeem. Surprised to seen him, she was tempted to ask him what he was doing in her neighbourhood.

"I swear I wasn't stalking you," Akeem jokingly said, with a chuckle.

"Come to think of it, I've never asked about you. You know, the whole scandal and all..."

"That's so kind of you. I was worried about you since you were the most affected," Akeem replied. His hands suddenly grabbed onto her waist.

Her shock wore away when an *okada* swerved close to her; he'd saved her from a potential accident. Her thanks were cut off by...

"Are you blind?" Akeem shouted at the *okada* rider, who neither looked back nor apologized.

Her heart was beating fast, Akeem's hands still on her waist. She should have told him off or put some distance between them, but she liked the firmness of his grip. They were in close proximity, and she could see the beads of sweat around his chiselled chin. A glance at his masculine arms almost made her drool again. He was wearing a sleeveless see-through shirt and shorts, and it was clear he was also returning from his own workout. Suddenly, he was becoming jacked up with muscles, and the veins popping out of his skin just made everything perfect.

"I'm so sorry," Akeem apologized, realizing he was holding her waist the whole time.

"It's okay," she whispered, swallowing for the third time. "Thanks for saving me."

"No problem. All these *okada* riders don't fear for their lives at all, yet they put other lives in danger."

"I'm sure he was delivering a package in the area. No motorbikes are allowed in this neighbourhood."

She didn't even know why she became attracted to him. Perhaps it was because she'd been fantasizing about them together. That could be the only reason. If not, she wouldn't be showing interest in a man younger than her.

"So, I will see you later," she blurted out.

"Wait." Akeem grabbed her hand.

"Hmmm," she hummed. He would need to stop

grabbing her anyhow, or else she might go insane from his touch.

"I was really worried about you when... when..." Akeem started, hesitated.

She knew he was referring to her miscarriage. "It's fine, I'm getting better now. I've been going to therapy, and I rarely cry lately..."

When she realized how chatty she had become about herself, she shut her mouth in an attempt to refrain from divulging personal matters.

"I'm happy. When I came the other day, your cook told me you were sick and refused to take your medications. Thankfully, my mother made you some herbs, and I have to thank your cook for accepting them."

"That was you?" Realizing it was the same herbs she drank that nursed her back to health. "I didn't know. Thank you!"

Akeem smiled. "You're welcome."

"Will meet at the office," she said and departed. She had a feeling that Akeem was watching her and tried not to look back until she was in her compound.

After that encounter, she couldn't stop thinking about him or not notice his presence in the office. The first thing she did upon arriving at work was drop her bag and linger around the accounts department. She noticed it made her staff a little tense, but she couldn't help it. But when her employees began to wonder if she had something important to tell the team or were worried that they weren't meeting expectations, she decided to drop by during lunchtime. She had also found her own behaviour absurd, cautioning herself most of the time, saying:

"Folake, you're not going crazy, are you? Oya! Stop this nonsense."

A few seconds later, she would head back in the direction of Akeem's office.

Fearing she was turning Akeem to her new obsession, she decided to bring it up in therapy.

"You're just lovesick," Doctor Titi diagnosed a while later.

"I don't love him," she disagreed, even though she hoped it was true.

"But you think about him all the time?"

"That's because I was moved by his kindness," she insisted. Nothing intimate or loving.

"How does he make you feel?" Doctor Titi asked curiously.

"My heart pounds whenever he's near me, and I sort of miss him, which I'm not supposed to."

"And that doesn't sound like love?"

"That's not love, doctor. He's much younger than me."

"So, if he's not younger than you, you could have given him a try?"

"I could've. He's got a perfect smile and good good-looking face. Oh my god! You should have seen his body these days. Not to talk of how kind and good he is to me…" Now she realized the way she felt about him. "Shit!"

Doctor Titi smiled, nodding retrospectively.

"You don't have to be ashamed of being in love. He's old enough to know the way you feel about him." Doctor Titi encouraged, insisting Folake profess her love to Akeem.

"I'm not going to embarrass myself, doctor. What if he does not see me that way? Imagine letting him know how I feel about him, and suddenly I find myself on the news, tainting my good name again."

"I understand. But you don't have to tell him right away. You can start seeing yourself being with him."

"How?" She was confused. "Don't chase that feeling away. Let it grow, and he will notice it himself, and if he feels the same way, he will surely reciprocate the feelings."

As crazy as it sounded, Folake chose to listen to her therapist's advice and not suppress her growing fondness for Akeem. To keep him closer to her, she would fake her own sickness, hoping he would take on the initiative of taking the wheels, and it worked. She knew he cared about her health, and with her *Oscar* performing skills, she had swooned him over but didn't have to try harder as he was ready to sacrifice himself for her comfort. They were usually the last to leave the office, and when no one was watching, she would drool, acting nicer compared to her usual self. She contemplated asking him over to her house on the weekend but didn't know how he would take it.

"Do you now live in my area?"

"Yes, I'm squatting with a friend. He and I are thinking of starting a startup very soon."

"That's nice! So you don't intend on staying longer with us?" She was happy for him, but at the same time felt sad as he would no longer be there at her beck and call. "What's your business idea?"

"We are venturing into digitizing real estate properties," he said curtly.

"Impressive! I didn't know you had it in you." She was somehow proud of him now. She had looked down on him in the past, only now she began to see him in a new light. "Is there a way I could help?"

"Not at all ma. We're presently working on our MVP, and we've pitched our ideas to some investors who have shown interest. But I appreciate your concern, ma," he replied.

"That's fine," she replied coolly, though hurt, she

managed to conceal her emotions.

"Ma, I could've asked for your help but I didn't want to disturb you."

"When will you stop calling me, 'ma'?"

"Ma?" Akeem cried, hitting the brakes at the same time.

Realizing how petty she sounded, she quickly said, "I mean, we've left work which means I'm no longer your boss."

"Ma, I...I..." Akeem stuttered.

She smiled, finding him more irresistibly.

"Folake is fine," she said, looking away.

"Alright, Folake," he whispered.

She was expecting him to resist calling her by her government name, anyone could have had a hard time adjusting to such a sudden request, but he just said her name with no fear at all, as if he had waited for it.

"Wow! Never knew you had such boldness in you?" she teased.

"You told me to. Is it not, Folake?"

She squinted as it sounded like he was the one having the most fun now.

"You know what? Screw it! Address me as your boss."

"You cannot take it back now."

They both burst into laughter until he blurted out what she never expected.

"Folake, can I take you out?"

She wasn't expecting him to take the first initiative of asking her out, but now that he did, she couldn't deny or reject such an offer. "Where do you want to take me?"

"I know a trendy restaurant on the Island, although I don't know if it will suit your rich palate."

"We'll see," she sighed.

She tried not to giggle each time she caught him steal glances at her through the rearview mirror. Their eyes met a couple of times. Folake couldn't get the confession out of her head. Even though he never said he liked her or was in love with her, because he asked her out, it made her feel like a teenager.

For their first date, she decided to visit the saloon to style her hair, carefully selected the outfit, and put a lot more consideration into her makeup by getting a makeup artist to do what she couldn't do for herself. Seeing her in her unusual state made Mr Aleshinloye happy, as she was blossoming like a newly planted flower, and he began to praise her.

"Oh, Mr Aleshinloye," she said bashfully and cleared her throat noisily.

"Will you be late? Should I wait up?" Mr Aleshinloye asked in a courteous voice.

"No, Mr Alesinlonye. I'm going out on a date."

Smiling, she swirled in her skater dress. She was wearing a dress for the first time in a long time; trousers, suits for formal, and jeans for casual were her daily wear. Akeem had asked her to wait in her house to be picked up and wouldn't want her to drive to their first date. He alerted her when he arrived in a *Toyota Camry*.

"I hope you don't mind it didn't have an AC?" Akeem asked nervously.

"It's comfortable," she replied, distracted by the green carpet.

She suddenly felt shy beside him and held her breath when he kissed her hand.

"I'm sorry, I should have asked for your consent first?" he said, carefully leaving her hand, but she clasped onto his hand, and he kissed her hand again, smiling with satisfaction as he drove into Eko Azure.

She looked up in surprise. A reservation at Eko Azure had to have been made for months. She eyed Akeem curiously. It was one of the newest restaurants and had twice been graced by ambassadorial guests and two A-list actresses. She linked her hand with his and walked into the restaurant that she had wanted to design. It was built dome-like, like *The Gherkin*, in London. Inside were tables set as hubs with palm frond roofs, with benches and marble floors in dark brown. The lanterns hanging from the ceiling appealed to her the most.

"Lovely," she said soon after they sat to eat in a restaurant that could have cost him a fortune.

"You can order anything," Akeem said, leaning forward. "After all, my boss paid my salary so I can pay for everything my Folake wants," he whispered.

She chuckled, completely swooned by him. She swallowed and ordered the least expensive thing.

She ended up teasing him for spending all his salary on her, but he didn't mind.

"Damn! We have to wait till next month for another fantastic date," Akeem teased her.

"Are you going to keep spending all your salaries on me?"

"Why not? Anything my Folake wants should be given to her," Akeem said casually.

She smiled as she cheekily said, "So, I'm also your boss and your Folake at the same time?"

They also spent their afternoons and evenings together, visiting more places she had never been to before but heard of. Then, one day, Akeem leaned over to her side - they had already driven into her compound – and waited to bid her good night. Her cook had already opened the door and was excitedly waiting for her.

"Would you mind being my girlfriend, Folake?" Akeem asked, his eyes searching.

She was stunned.

A long, tense moment passed before she replied.

"No, I wouldn't mind."

He lowered his gaze to her lips; his lips descended on hers and, for a few seconds, wouldn't leave hers. It was sensual and sexual at the same time, triggering her neediness to take things further with him.

"Good night," he murmured, his eyes fixed on her.

"Good night," she replied. Her legs had turned liquid and a little uneasy, and she had wet her her panties. She didn't want to let him go just like that but was relieved when he helped her unfasten her belt and stepped out to open the door for her.

When she slid out of the car, Akeem gave her a peck on the cheek before driving away.

She ran up the stairs, giggling, and buried herself under the duvet, screaming with joy. Her heart and belly tingled with love, and it felt unreal that she had found love again.

27

As days turned to weeks, Folake vested her time on her rendezvous with Akeem. She was impatient with his steady pace, but she missed him every second he was away. She also realised she wasn't only comfortable with him but felt secure enough to share her fears. Unlike Folarin, and a couple of other dates in the past, he was willing to wait until she was ready even though she was already ready to go third base with him.

Each time Akeem said, 'You have such beautiful

eyes,' she felt the need to wear mascara to accentuate them. She now wore less foundation and because he stared at her lips a lot, she now wore red lipstick.

She woke up dreamy and went to bed the same way each day after reading the messages Akeem sent her.

One day during their date, while he was toying with her hair, he asked:

"Do you know I was drawn to you from the day I met you?"

She said nothing as she was struggling with the wetness in her extremities and her longing to kiss him. Luckily, he didn't seem to notice as he continued.

"I just thought it was because you were the first woman that was beside me after a long time. I was so distracted that your voice woke me up. It was strange, and I liked the sound of it enough to enter your car without suspicion."

She sat up. "I agree. I have never trusted a man to get into my car, much less a stranger, but I didn't have any fear."

"I think it was fate," Akeem murmured and pulled her back into his embrace.

She almost guffawed. Her mother had mentioned that she didn't mind if she had brought a mechanic, maybe it was fate. She wondered what her mother would think now but then it didn't matter. He was an accountant. And he was impossible to resist. She had fallen under his spell and if it was fate then it was doing a good job of keeping her distracted.

"I was very ashamed of myself that day I saw you, but I couldn't resist you not helping me. I just didn't want you to see me in a negative way, so I retracted."

She pulled back from him and turned so she could read his face.

"When we met again. I knew I had to do everything to get you to see me. When I heard of your strange request, I accepted it. I knew if there was anyone who would be the mother of my children, it would be you."

She sighed with relief. When she met him, he was in desperate need, and she thought he could have mistakenly taken her kindness for love.

"What has changed now?"

"Because of your green light. Damn! I was worried some lucky bastard would take you from me. I was close to giving up."

"What's so special about me?" she hauntingly muttered.

"What's not special about you? Everything about you is beautiful, and you're the most beautiful woman I have ever seen in my life," he assured her again, taking her face in his hand to kiss her lips until she was dizzy.

Last week, Akheem walked into her office with an excuse of having a file for her to look through and drew her to him, her body matching his as they got lost in each other's eyes. They were about to kiss when Emma opened the door, catching them in the act, rendering them helpless to convince her otherwise.

She had become used to his touches and kisses, carelessly ignoring the fact that they were in her office and anyone could walk in on them. Since they had never been caught before, this had made them so comfortable and relaxed.

Emma's wide-open eyes and mouth caused her to rethink, especially as Akheem stood awkwardly near her stiffened body and seemed unsure of what to say to Emma, who was now smiling sheepishly at them.

She nudged him out with the folder he had walked in with and was pleasantly surprised when he blew her a kiss before closing the door.

"I knew it!" Emma chanted, giggling and doing a funny dance.

"*Knew* what? It's not what you think," she denied, looking away.

"Oh, it's exactly what I think. I thought as much when you were being inquisitive about him a couple of weeks ago," Emma insisted.

"Me?" she asked, confused.

"Yes, you! You asked me if he could be dating someone or seeing someone."

"I did?" she asked, frowning. "That can't be possible."

"Yes, you did. And now it makes sense that you're

dating him now."

She watched Emma recreate the scene of the day she had mentioned and then began talking to her boss.

She wondered if she'd been that obvious, Akeem was her subordinate and much younger than her. She didn't want to lose the respect of her employees. And feared Akeem would be subjected to another scandal or unfair treatment because of their relationship.

"Just don't tell anyone you saw us," she warned.

Emma nodded.

She glared at Emma.

"I promise!" Emma swore. "But it's nice seeing you both happy. He was very worried about you during those times and would always ask after you."

"He did?" she asked in surprise.

"Yes, even when he was being stalked by some idiots, he was only worried about you." Emma dramatically waved the files she was holding.

It was her first time hearing such a thing. Akeem never told her about being stalked. He left the part but only showed interest in her well-being.

"I didn't know that. How come he never told me that?" she murmured distractedly.

"Probably because he only cares about you, and I'm glad you've also realized that."

Realizing he had always shown his concern since the beginning, it took her a long time to acknowledge it. Folake was grateful she managed to muster some courage to accept him if not she would have missed out on good love.

Akeem's love language was something new. Most of the men she had dated in the past were much older or her age mates, and they all had something in common. She was the lover bird in every relationship she had, would spend the most, cater to their needs, and even withstood their passive insults in their attempt to belittle her.

Akeem, thirteen years younger than her, bought her flowers and several thoughtful gifts and came over to her house just to cook for her and listen to her when the cook was away. He didn't seem to expect something in return. She loved every experience with him, believed in herself and discovered herself even more.

In order to reward him, she invited him over to spend the night in her house and prayed she could keep herself composed.

28

It had only been one month since Folake and Akeem started dating but she felt like she had known him for years. For their one-month anniversary, she sent Mr Aleshinloye and her cook on a two-day trip, all expenses paid. She made sure to prepare herself and a full-course meal they would be having, herself being the main dish of the night. In her see-through lace robe, she opened the door, expecting to see Akeem so she could jump at him.

"What are you doing here?" she asked Folarin, annoyed and clumsily covering herself.

Folarin tried to kiss her.

She instinctively slapped him. She had always wanted to slap some sense in him, and it felt good afterwards.

"What's wrong with you? I thought you were prepared for me?" he said, holding his cheek in his hand and gesturing with the other.

"Prepared for you? Did I know you were coming?"

"Come on, don't be like that. I know you miss me," he drew her closer to himself. She wasn't having it at all and pushed him away. "Trust me, I also came packing," he flexed.

"Folarin, you have to leave." She got worked up, anxiously thinking Akeem wouldn't meet him there, so he wouldn't have another opinion about her.

"Are you expecting a guest?"

"Yes, so leave before he shows up." She forcefully pushed him and opened the door, expecting him to take clues and walk out on his own.

"He? You now have a boyfriend? How can you be cheating on me?" He pompously assumed they were in some sort of relationship, and it was news to her ear. "Cheating on you? Are we in a relationship?"

"We are. I suddenly returned, and now you're with another guy. How loose can you be?" Folake felt like slapping him again, but she would rather not have things escalate. "Folarin, you and I were done twenty years ago. Don't come here thinking you will have your way to my heart again.”

"I never said we are done!”

"So? Disappearing and reappearing all the time like a ghost, do you think I'll call that relationship? Where were you twenty years ago, Folarin?”

"I was in the States, and you know that,” he snapped back.

"You were in the States, and I was pregnant with your child. Where were you when I needed you the most?”

Folarin pulled back, looking surprised.

She swallowed her saliva and continued, "At my worst time, you weren't there, Folarin.”

Folarin stretched his hands toward her. "You had our child?”

"You deserted me, and I was hopeless, thinking of committing suicide, but now I realized that the best decision of my life was getting rid of that pregnancy.”

"You did what?” Folarin staggered and then came at her in a rage.

She sneered. Although she was relieved to have confessed, she had no intention of repeating herself.

"You killed my child? You stand there boldly –”

"You discarded me. I didn't know you were travelling. We were together the day before you left, and you –” she inhaled sharply and rubbed her burning chest. Her therapist was the one who encouraged her to let go of whatever she was hoarding and let her feelings be known, but the reaction she was expecting from him was rather a nonchalant one since he never really cared about her.

"You killed my only hope in life?" Folarin growled.

Was he really expecting her to apologize for something her mother forced her to do? She scoffed and turned into Folarin's hand, gripping her throat.

"Folarin, stop it. You're hurting me," she cried out, struggling to break free from his grip.

"Do you have any idea what you've done, Folake? You murdered a being and just casually said it out without any remorse."

She managed to slip her hand between his and her throat. "You don't get to judge me, Folarin. My body, my choice."

"I thought you were different from the rest. That you have some sense in you, but now you've proven me wrong."

"Are you telling me I'd rather had the baby of a man that jilted me?"

"Yes, since that's what good women do. You were supposed to keep my seed and raise it. Maybe, one day I will return like now and claim the both of you. But you dare tell me you had an abortion? Have you gone mad?"

The twitch in his eyes confirmed her fears, and in that distraction, he pulled her hand off and tightened his grip. She fought him, but his grip was firm as he pinned her to the chair.

She heard a muffled thud and then her neck felt free.

She opened her eyes then though her vision was hazy but she could make out and sighed with relief. Folarin was sitting on the floor and nursing his jaw and Akeem's fingers were balled into fists.

"Is he your boyfriend?" Folarin bellowed.

"I don't care who you are. Just don't hurt her," Akeem warned.

Folarin scrambled to his feet.

"Have you told him who I am to you?"

She hissed, her eyes fixed on Akeem.

"Folake, are you okay?" Akeem asked in a soft voice.

Her throat was sore, so she nodded.

"Did he also know what you did to my child?"

Folarin looked alarmed when she called the police.

"I will never forgive you for what you did to me," Folarin said, moving close to the door. " Never! You may have your little boyfriend protecting you now, but I'll always return to take my revenge."

Akeem had to run to Folake's aid as she was almost fainting after the deadly encounter. She was close to death just now, and the person she never expected to threaten her life showed her his true colour.

"Are you okay?" Akeem asked again, helping her up.

To her relief, he didn't ask who Folarin was to her. He took her to her bedroom upstairs, gave her warm water to drink, and then sat beside her on the bed, his hand brushing her hair.

"Let's visit the police station tomorrow," Akeem said.

She nodded.

She felt bad that their evening was ruined, but he assured her it was fine.

"Just make sure you get some rest."

When Folake expressed her fear of Folarin showing up again, Akeem stayed with her. With Mr Alesinloye and the cook away, Akeem had to stay. He drove her to work two days later, acting like the bodyguard she employed. The fright she suffered left a permanent scar in her, as she would constantly peek around her surroundings, expecting something or someone to pop up; this feeling made her so uneasy that by Wednesday, she hurried to her therapist to get a prescription for calming pills.

"Doctor, you don't understand how I'm feeling. Sometimes, I feel as if he's watching me take every step."

She was very unsettled and would often scratch her head in distress. She thought after sleeping it over that fateful night, she would have gotten better. Instead, she woke up with another trauma.

"I don't want you to get addicted to the drugs, Miss Folake. Why don't we work things out without it?"

"How, Doctor?" She scratched her head in confusion. "I just need those drugs to find my peace. I won't get addicted to it."

"If that is so, I'll put you on one. Before that, can you

explain what that moment felt like?"

"He was...he wanted to kill me..." She was out of it as she spoke, not even sure of her own words. "He could've killed me, and I don't know why he's become that way." She explained better after drinking some water.

"Have you reported it to the police?"

"Yes, but they didn't take my case seriously." She was at the police station that afternoon with Akeem, but because that wasn't her first time making such reports, they had judged her for having dangerous men lurking around her.

"That's so sad. I'll encourage you to be prepared anytime. Miss Folake, look at me." She got closer to Folake, holding her by the shoulder as she was about to get candid with her. "I'm also a survivor of an abusive relationship, and I know how scary it is to be in that situation. You have to decode yourself from that fear of the unknown, take control of your mind and fear, and don't forget to protect yourself."

Doctor Titi's words pacified her, healing her the right way. Since she also understood being in that fearful state, Folake felt assured to tackle her own fear. She needed to stop dwelling on negativity and focus on her recovery.

"I don't think I will be needing those antidepressants any longer, Doctor. Thank you," she said after calming down.

29

In spite of everything Bimpe had done to her, causing her the greatest harm of losing her *needed* pregnancy, Folake decided to pay her a visit. She had reasoned many ways to get back at Bimpe over her betrayal, but she couldn't bear to take Bimpe as her enemy. She knew it wasn't her intention to cause her harm.

That weekend, as she left the Island for the Mainland, hoping to reunite with her long-lost sister, it wasn't to convince Bimper to divorce Femi.

"Whatever you choose to do with your life now shouldn't be any of my concern. But I want to make it known that I have forgiven you for everything. It wasn't your fault, neither was it mine."

Bimpe broke into uncontrollable tears.

Still hurt, she didn't rush to her side to comfort her.

"I just couldn't forgive myself, Aunty Folake."

It's Aunty Folale now, Folake mused, still hurt yet sympathetic. It was clearly seen from her appearance how wrecked and damaged she was. Even the house was mirroring her aura, a complete catastrophe. Femi had laid his hands on her again, as one could see some fresh bruises evenly displayed on her face and body, and it weakened Folake even more, but she dared not mention her divorce.

"Bimpe, my life lately has been nothing but good, and that is because I have taken control of it. You're right. I'm not married like you, so I don't know what marriage should be. But one thing I know for sure is that our generation does not have any excuses not to choose the right things for ourselves."

She paused to keep her pace, swallowing her saliva and tears.

"I want you all to be happy. Look at your sons, the state they're in, and it's because their mother chose such a life for them. What if they grow up to become like their fathers one day?"

Instantly, Bimpe went on her knees and began to beg

her. "Please let bygone be bygone. I'll not betr-"

"No, I won't do that anymore. Bimpe, you can't even free yourself from this abusive man, and we've seen how dangerous he is when you were living with me. I'll not stand in your way or his again."

"Aunty Folake, I've learned my lesson. That man will kill me one day if you don't help me," Bimpe begged.

She stared at Bimpe's arms around her leg and sighed. Sbe wasn't that desperate to have anyone back in her life, so she bent down and untangled Bimpe's arms from her leg.

"I have forgiven you, Bimpe," she said to calm Bmpe down while assisting Bimpe up, helping her wipe her tears with a handkerchief. "However, I'm not your salvation."

"If you really need help, I'll introduce you to my therapist. Don't worry about any payment, just attend your sessions with her, and I can assure you that the decision you will make for yourself will always come through you."

And if you ever take on the boldness and I'll help you secure a job again,

She left but cried on her way, remembering how tied to the past she had been and hoping Bimpe would take a leap for the sake of the children, if not for herself. Femi would come up with more tricks again, and since he had the support of his own mother, Bimpe might have a hard time seeing the light.

In less than five months, she would be forty years old. She decided to call Emma to find out how the plans for her extravagant birthday was going, as she hadn't brought it up again. But as soon as she stepped out of her car, she sensed something was different in her house. As soon as she tossed the thought out, Mama Rere got up. From her mother's attire – *gele* twice the size of her head, wrists and neck laden with jewellery and *aso oke* – she knew her mother had attended a wedding.

"Maami," she courtesied.

"I'm just coming from my friend's daughter's wedding. The youngest daughter, the one who just graduated a couple of months ago. God knows when they will come to celebrate with me, too."

Mama Rere had many friends to even count, and every weekend was a party or event to attend.

"Folake, how long should I wait for you to bring a man home?" she asked disappointedly.

"I've found one already," she bragged.

"Who?"

"He has given me peace of mind," she said and bit her lips before she could add 'and makes me feel loved.'

"Then bring him home to meet us."

"He's younger than me."

"At your age, you shouldn't be picky. Instead, be grateful you've found one," Mama Rere said.

At this point, she thought of confronting her mother

about the past, and out of the blue.

"You know that if I had had that baby, you would not be clamouring for a grandchild."

"I did what every mother would have done. How can I allow an unwanted pregnancy to hinder you from finishing school?"

"But you don't like the fact that I focus on work. You, of all people, believe that a woman shouldn't aspire to do much for herself, only focus on getting a man and having a child."

Mama Rere suddenly became silent.

"Did Daddy even know about the abortion?" she abruptly asked.

"Was he supposed to know?" Mama Rere asked.

She turned to her mother. "He's supposed to know, after all, he is my father."

"What else could he have done if he knew? You will only end up disappointing him further."

"How can I be a disappointment when he's the one sleeping around with multiple women, leaving you to take care of his -"

Mama Rere slapped her.

There was a sudden silence between them as they glared at each other menacingly.

"You should never disrespect your father in his absence and in my presence," Mama Rere warned.

It took all she had in her not to slap her mother back.

She didn't need this type of anger, but she was also tired of keeping it in.

"Did I lie? He was like that, and you knew and did nothing about it," she said, her voice raising. She dodged another slap.

"And so what? Did the world end because I did what a loving wife should do?" Mama Rere fired back.

"So pretending not to know about his affairs is what a good woman does? You could've confronted him, raged at him, thrown bottles or anything at him, not cried yourself to sleep and wondered why he doesn't find you sexually attractive anymore. The worst that could've happened should have been a divorce."

"That is what you children of nowadays are doing. In my days, a good woman would look the other way and focus on her family," she defended.

"Is that why you, of all people, advised Bimpe to accept her husband back? Do you even know he has laid his hands on her again? Is it when that girl dies in his hand that you and your sister will realize what wickedness you're committing against that child?"

Mama Rere hissed. "She will not die. A good woman must persevere and pray for her family. Even Reverend said it was the devils at work, trying to break the two of them apart."

"The same reverend you brought the other day to sleep with me? Does that one even know his wrong from right?"

No matter how she tried talking Mama Rere out of believing in this same man of God, it all fell on deaf ears. Her mother became a fervent believer when her father started misbehaving. Mama Rere would attend all series of vigils, convinced that her prayer was what was needed to save her husband from the spirit of fornication. For years, she fasted and prayed and now believed her prayers worked since he was no longer chasing after women.

"A woman must be prayerful and submissive to her husband. Once you get married, you too will realize the reason why Bimpe is also trying to protect hers," Mama Rere insisted.

"No, mommy. Bimpe will realize she's not a fool that can be manipulated by your blindness and do what is right for herself and her boys."

Mama Rere instantly got annoyed, "Don't tell me you're still putting this nonsense in her head? Are you trying to destroy her joy? So she could become like you, a failure?"

"Mommy, what you don't realize is that remarriage is possible after divorce, and there will be plenty of men rushing to her after leaving that douchebag of a man."

Mama Rere gawked at her, dumbfounded.

She scoffed. Mama Rere's ideology of marriage was that as a woman, you only marry once and die in that marriage. The terms 'remarriage and divorce' were strictly frowned upon by her church, and any woman who was either divorced or remarried would get isolated from their gatherings.

"God forbid what you wish for your sister-in-law. Aren't you ashamed to be thinking like the devil himself?" Mama asked in a pleading voice.

"The only devil close to you is that reverend deceiving you all in that church, and I will not stand still and watch you or your sister destroy Bimpe's life," she finished and left for her room upstairs.

She had to make sure Bimpe took the advice she offered; she picked up her phone and began to dial the number, then stopped herself.

"Bimpe has to love herself enough to want to leave," she sighed. "Bimpe, please take that step. I'll be waiting for you."

The Women Entrepreneurship Scheme confirmed that Folake was a recipient of the award and apologized for any misunderstandings. Soon after, Forbes asked to appear on the cover of their magazine.

She had also agreed to her Forbes cover; after all, all her hard work and dedication brought her this recognition, and she deserved it. The airport project and the palace rebuilding were going fine. They had also received multiple projects, both at home and abroad. Being the inheritor of a refined manor had caught the attention of many overseas buyers.

There had been those proposing some insane amount of money to possess the estate; some wanted the manor and the estate, and it made her wonder what the difference was amidst paying inheritance tax, which, fortunately, Bill Carson had prepared for her. When the noise from emails and phone calls became unbearable, she decided to keep the property.

The only person left in that gigantic house was Bill Carson's butler; the rest of the house workers had quit their jobs after finding out who would be the new lady of the house. For a person of her colour, she was looked down upon by people whom Bill Carson had trusted to look after her needs. The butler had been doing a great job managing the house and gave her enough feedback to make her reward him.

She planned to visit the UK with Akeem. She looked forward to a romantic getaway in times like this. He had also proposed taking her to meet his family, most especially his mother, who hadn't met her life-saver yet.

"Do you think they will like me?" she worriedly asked.

"What's there to hate?" Akeem asked, smiling as he stared into her eyes.

"I'm old," she said dauntingly, but he teased that she hadn't lived a century.

"You're only thirteen years older than me. You're still very young," Akeem tried to convince her. "I find you charming and cute."

"Has your type been older women?" she teased.

"Not at all, but I don't have enough evidence to prove myself now," Akeem joked.

She chuckled.

Ever since Akeem came into her life, it had all been laughter and joy. She had even grown younger in mind and body, and she didn't have to hate herself or her body when she was with him. The first time they had the relationship consummated was a week after Folarin's attack.

She never expected how Akeem loved her body; in fact, she was stunned by how he made her feel. Turned out she wasn't the one with the problem but Folarin. It had been three weeks since his threats of returning to take his revenge, but no one knew where he was. She had hired some private investigators to fish out Folarin's whereabouts, but there was no news of where he was yet. Her greatest fear was him showing up like a ghost at a time when she wouldn't be expecting, just as he usually does.

As expected of him, he showed up to her office unannounced, and at that moment, she had let her guard down completely.

30

Folarin barged into Folake's office while she was having a Zoom meeting.

"I… I tried," Emma started and mouthed, "Should I call the police?"

She was about to come up with an excuse to end the Zoom meeting when the commissioner said, "Meeting adjourned."

She closed her laptop and looked up.

"I'm only here to talk," Folarin said as he slid into one of the chairs facing her.

"You may leave," she urged Emma, but she worried

something might happen in her absence, but she braced herself by crossing her arms. "It's okay, Emma. Leave it to me."

"Folake…" Folarin started and leaned forward.

She inhaled sharply as she pulled back, holding onto that fateful night so fear wouldn't eat her up.

"I'm sorry for how I handled the situation last time. It wasn't my intention to hurt you, but you only made me mad, and I had no choice," Folarin said in a condescending way.

"You had no choice? What other choices do you have to hurt me?"

"Folake, you had no right to abort my child. That should have been our child," Folarin continued arrogantly.

"You expect me to keep and raise a fatherless baby?" she felt insulted by his arrogance. "Weren't you married with kids?"

"Those are not my children. They are my wife's, and I can't father a child anymore. So you can imagine how upset I am that you killed my only heir."

"And what makes you not be able to father a child?" she asked, not because she cared but to better understand him.

"I had prostate cancer a few years before meeting my ex-wife. And I was rendered impotent after the treatment. Thankfully, she already had children of her own, and it wasn't a problem not being able to father one."

She saw the twitch in his face and wondered if he expected her to show some empathy like she usually did.

Unfazed and unbothered, she asked, "So what is my fault in this?"

Folarin gawked at her.

"Folake, you've changed," Folarin murmured a while later. "I'm sure that your younger boyfriend has been putting ideas in your head, manipulating you to be another person entirely."

"Please, don't bring Akeem into this. The only insane person here is you, spewing nonsense out of your mouth," she scolded.

"I'm telling you what you did was wrong. Instead of apologizing to me right away, you're forming in my presence. Or don't I deserve some apology?"

She scoffed at his ridiculousness. How come all the men in her life, all except Akeem, speak from the same vocabulary?

"Folarin, you have yet to apologize to me, but you want my own apology? How low of you to think you're worth more."

She observed Folarin as he stood up from his seat, talking and gesturing wildly, looking back at her at intervals. A while later, with sank into the chair, looking deflated.

"Folake, I'm here to give us a chance. You and I are

mature intellectual beings who go well together. We can get married and probably adopt a child to raise together in the future." Folarin gestured.

She laughed humourlessly. "Me? Get married to you? Aren't you a dreamer?"

"You told me you've passed the age of men seeking your hands in marriage. I'm even doing you a favour here by offering myself to you. We can get married next month, and I'm sure your mother will love that."

She smiled, welled with pride and said, "Well, for your information, I don't need to beg a man to marry me. I'm beautiful enough for any man, and he must be lucky to have me as a wife."

She walked to the middle of the room and stood in a pose.

"Look at me. I'm flawless, I'm above the standard, and I'm rich. If I want a man from Asia, Europe, America, or even this Africa, I can easily find them for a buck. I don't chase anymore. I now attract." She was so stunned by her declaration that she decided to finish it with the flick of her braids.

"Aren't you even ashamed of dating someone younger than you?" Folarin asked in a spiteful tone.

"Why should I? He's good-looking, loving, and kind to me. And most importantly, he's quite fantastic in bed more than you are."

She smiled and stood akimbo. She was finally free of Folarin. She had longed to say those words face to face with this enemy and was victorious. She had finally freed herself from his captivity, both the past and present, and she was no longer afraid of him.

In that excitement, she marched to the door and opened it.

"Get out of my office and my life, Folarin. It's time to bid each other farewells."

Folarin didn't move. "We can only be done if I say so," Folarin insisted, crossing his arms and smiling.

Seeing his resistance and knowing how her security guards fawned over him, she was relieved to see police officers march towards her with Emma. Folarin resisted, but they dragged him out, escorted by her legal team while she linked hands with Emma and jumped excitedly.

Akeem went into her office with a tub of her favourite ice cream. She smiled, closed her laptop and walked into his embrace.

"I'm so proud of you," Akeem whispered in her ear.

She giggled and moved away from him.

"You never cease to surprise me, you beautiful, wonderful soul," Akeem said.

And, of course, she was the most proud of herself; after all, her pain in the ass had been sorted, and she would never have to revisit the past again.

She called Ijeoma as soon as Akeem left her office.

She also called to inform Ijeoma about her newly

found love, and she couldn't be more than happier for her friend.

"I would love to meet him one day," Ijeoma said. "All these good things I keep hearing about him. He's perfect for you."

"I believe so," she replied. They discussed important issues and gossip. Their friend, Felicia had gotten divorced from her rich husband, but the craziest part of the story was how she managed to walk away with half of his properties when she was guilty of infidelity.

"Is there even a law that supports such?"Ijeoma asked, baffled and marvelling at the whole issue.

"If she has enough evidence against him, I think it's possible," she agreed. "But such is life. I can't even imagine that Felicia knew of such a strategy, but she would be the first to advocate for long-lasting marriages. I didn't even know she was capable of extramarital affairs."

"Always give the benefit of the doubt to some people. They may not be who they preach to be. Imagine that reverend instigating Bimpe to stay married to her abuser. I can't even fathom why these women listen to such people?"

Ijeoma hissed in agreement, baffled for the same reason. "That reminds me of my mother-in-law. Can you imagine she told my husband to stop financing my PhD?"

"Why? Isn't she also a professor?" she asked in

horror.

"Exactly. She said I might become too educated for her son, and that may not seem right in people's eyes."

She shook her head. "She is the last person I'd expect to show her displeasure at such an achievement. I mean, she is the first woman to head the Department of Further Mathematics in a state-owned university. I thought she was supposed to lead by example?"

"Example? It's way easier to say than to accept. Many of these older generation women are sort of jealous of the younger ones. Seeing we can make a family and also hold career baffles most of them."

She frowned. Ijeoma summarized what Doctor Titi had mentioned during one of their sessions. She wasn't able to comprehend the discussion she had with her mother over her father's unfaithfulness and how her mother had lived till now, bearing the secrets of her knowing about the affairs.

"It could be because she is more ashamed of knowing than confronting the situation," Doctor Titi explained. "Being a woman of those times, there weren't any forms of resistance happening as it is now. You can imagine how monolithic they were those days."

"But she could free herself now, couldn't she?"

"If she believes she's hurt, she could. Although for people like that, they sometimes take their frustration out on the children, rather than facing the situation."

It now made sense why Mama Rere could only show nothing

but displeasure of her daughter. No matter how hard she tried, she would never be good enough in her Mama Rere's eyes.

"Do you think I will be able to forgive her?" she asked sullenly. She wasn't even sure if she was ready to let go of every pain, hurtful word, and constant belittlement her mother inflicted on her.

"I believe it starts with you forgiving yourself. It's not your fault, Miss Folake. You're never in the wrong, but to forgive your mother, it has to start with you," Doctor Titi has said.

"I think I'll give it time," she murmured thoughtfully. Perhaps, she could get her mother to go for therapy. Going to therapy had become her favourite hobby now. It was as if Doctor Titi knew all the answers to her problems and had a magical spell that healed all her pains. Doctor Titi also praised her for pardoning Bimpe for what she did, mentioning how Bimpe had also been showing up to therapy.

"She reminds me of you when you first came here. A soul that has lost its identity and emotions. I'm so happy you led her here."

"How is she decoding life?"

"One after the other. She's getting better and has even shown interest in one of our domestic violence outreach. She wishes to start writing again." Doctor Titi was aware of her responsibility to never disclose or discuss another patient's private conversation, but because Folake recommended Bimpe and their friendship that had grown.

"She could write?" she blurted out in surprise.

"Yes, in fact, she said she wanted to become a fictional writer when she was little, but her parents had frowned on such an act."

"I'm so grateful for your help, Doctor. You're saving lives here, and I don't know if I could donate for more women to attend your sessions?"

"That will be lovely. We also run a charity cause here, and I promise that your donation will be used for greater causes."

She wrote a check of twenty million naira before taking her leave. She wished her donation reached women who were battling with domestic abuse and stigmatization; that way, many would regain their self-confidence much like she did.

"Folake, what's on your mind?" Ijeoma asked. "You've been quiet."

"A big fortieth birthday and an NGO."

"Should I get the name and registration ready?" Emma asked *as soon as she sat by her desk the next day.*

"What shall we even call it?" she wondered. *She would want a name that represented her reason. Perhaps it was best to wait until Ijeoma joined them.*

"How about the term - it's my decision?"

"Sounds intriguing! Let's call it that.," she agreed. *"How did you come up with such a name now?"*

"Because it should be our decision. I know it will do a lot of women good, and the name just sounds right."

"Wow, what changed?" she asked, wearing a proud smile.

"Life changes, Boss." Emma smiled back.

"NGO!?" Ijeoma exclaimed. "I've been thinking about that for some time. We should rub minds."

"We should. I talked about it with Emma. Something

to benefit women. Emma has been asking about what we should call it?"

"It's not fair. Emma has stolen my friend," Ijeoma feigned, bawling.

"Don't be jealous. Just come and stay the holiday, and she won't steal me away."

"And be the third with Akeem there? No way!"

"Na your loss."

"Na, you know. Listen, I'll be handling your birthday bash, so tell Emma to lay off. Good night."

"Okay Ma," she said, giggling. "Good night."

31

Out of all her employees, Folake expected Akeem to be willing to relocate to the new office site with her. Instead, Akeem had tendered his resignation letter to her that morning, and his reasons were that he and his co-founder had secured a heavy investment and would have to travel to America.

"Why now?" Folake complained. "I'm happy for you and so proud of you, but I don't just understand why you need to leave for America."

Her worries were not about him finding his own path,

but it could mean they might no longer be an item.

"I would love to bring you along with me, but my suitcase is quite small," Akeem teased in a soft voice.

She wasn't interested in his joking about a serious situation.

"I'll miss you," Akeem said, drawing her closer.

"I don't believe you. You're going to America, where there will be a lot of beautiful women."

"And who said they are beautiful? When I'm dating the most beautiful woman in the whole world."

Although Akeem always knew how to please her and make her feel better with his words, he would have to do more to convince her of his sincerity. This was a big change in her new life.

"It's just for a year," Akeem tried to assure her. "And after that we will return to the country."

She wouldn't want to be a happiness wrecker and it wasn't her nature to make a scene out of any situation, so she accepted the fate without further questioning. Before his departure, they mostly spent time together, going on dates and sleeping over at each other's houses.

She had met his mother and sister, and they were lovely beings who didn't frown at their union. She didn't have to reduce her worth or self to please Akeem's family. Instead, they had taken her as a family and confidant.

She had yet to bring Akeem over to meet her own parents because she was afraid of their intruding on her relationship. She knew Mama Rere might frustrate Akeem, putting the ideas of marriage in his head, which might destroy her relationship with him. It hadn't been long since they realized their feelings for each other, so the idea of marriage was a no-no for her to bring into conversation.

She drove him to the airport herself, and there she met Akeem's cofounder. He was also of the same age as Akeem, vibrant and full of life. Compared to the two, she felt like their guardian, seeing them off and quite embarrassed when Akeem displayed his affection for her with kisses on her cheeks and forehead.

Ten minutes before his departure, Akeem sneaked a handwritten note in her bag, telling her to open it when she was alone, and when the time for their departure reached, he wouldn't want to let go of her hands after giving her a long passionate kiss.

"I wish I could take you with me," Akeem sighed, kissing her hands.

She was thinking the same thing and holding back tears, replied, "I wish I could come along."

"Oya nah! You people should hurry up!" Akeem's friend and business partner cried.

"Bro, give me a minute," Akeem said, still looking at her. "I want you to always be happy and I promise to always call."

Akeem kissed her, and she pulled back, encouraging

him to head for the departure gate; he kept looking back, and she wouldn't stop waving at him.

"I promise, okay?" Akeem until he was out of sight.

When she was driving out of the airport, she felt her feelings overpower her. She was missing him already, and if she could run back to stop him from leaving, she could have. She read the note he sneaked into her bag. It was a note, telling her what she meant to him; whatever happens, he would always choose her, and his love for her would never change.

"I'm not supposed to be feeling this way, but I can't help it," she said to her therapist two days after of Akeem's departure. She said to her therapist after two days of Akeem's departure.

"Are you afraid he's going to be like the rest?"

"Yes," she said dispiritedly. Folarin and the rest had shown her their worst sides, and now her fear was Akeem doing the same thing.

"Would you want to trust him?" Doctor Titi asked.

"Yes, I want to give it a try and see where this leads," she replied. And she was right for believing him; every day, Akeem would call. He had settled in quite well in the States, and everything was going great for their startup and his partner. For hours they would talk on the phone whether both were occupied with their own work or tired from work.

A month before her fortieth birthday, she received the

most shocking news of her life. She had dreamt of receiving an insane gift that made her the happiest person, then waking up to realize that she could be pregnant. Over the weeks, she had worked herself sore, finally settling in the new office complex, and was preparing for the entrepreneurship award ceremony happening two weeks before her birthday. She hadn't seen her period that previous month but never thought it could be worth being suspicious of. But when she became frequently fatigued, flash dizziness and tenderness of her breasts, she hurried to her gynaecologist.

"Congratulations, Miss Folake," her doctor said, "You're two months pregnant."

This time, she didn't have to labour to have a baby; it happened naturally and freely. It was unexpected to think that something like that could happen to her without having to labour for it. Not only would she be having a baby, but she would also have a man in her life.

Her first thought was to call to let Akeem know about the pregnancy, but something changed her mind, making her reconsider whether he might receive the news the same way she did. After all, they weren't planning on having a child.

"What if that hinders him from what he's doing?" she complained to Ijeoma that night.

"I see no reason not to tell the man responsible for

it," Ijeoma had replied.

"He's grown, Folake. Stop treating your baby's father like a child."

"I know he's not a child, but don't you think the news might come as a shock to him?" she contemplated.

"Remember, Folake, you're both dating. This time, you did not pay him any dime to have his child."

"But…" Above everything, she feared to break the pregnancy news to Akeem or anybody apart from Ijeoma. Her last miscarriage taught her a great lesson: to always keep to herself so the devil will not manifest his deeds again.

"But they will find out when you start showing, won't they?"

"Yes, but I'm not making it a big deal like last time."

"You may not want to, but you have a big birthday celebration coming up."

"But…"

"It's okay. Emma will help so you can cut down on work. If you're worried, don't take new projects."

"That's true," she said.

"That's why I'm the wise one."

"Ah!?"

"Good night. Speak tomorrow."

She chuckled and spread herself out to bed, daydreaming about Akeem as she drifted to sleep.

It was almost six in the morning when Mama Rere's call woke her. She found her calling bothersome and worried she might have sensed her pregnancy from afar. If not, there was no reason to call this early.

"Shit!" she cussed, holding her head in her hand as she sat numb on the bed. Her eyes were tired and she had woken up with a headache, yet her phone kept ringing beside her nonstop, aggravating her even more as she wished it would stop ringing so she could go back to sleep.

"Mommy, what is it?" she asked sternly when she finally picked up, expressing her displeasure. Her mother's voice faded on the phone, like she was terrified of something. "Mommy, you have to speak up because I'm very tired."

"Folake, what are we going to do?" Mama Rere murmured, sounding hysterical.

"What happened?" She readjusted to a sitting position and waited for Mama Rere to continue. "It's your brother."

"Who's that?" She guessed it could be Femi, so she remained unalarmed and unhinged. All news about him was always bad news anyways.

"He was arrested last night by the police."

And so what? "He probably did something to deserve it," she sighed and lay back in bed.

"He killed someone!"

"What?" Folake flung herself out of the bed, almost passed out by her mother's confession. "Femi did what?"

"It was all devil's work. He didn't mean to," Mama Rere said. "Mommy, killing someone is not something that just easily happens like that."

Suddenly, something stuck to her, her mind searching for answers after remembering Bimpe, hesitating to ask if his victim was the same person they knew.

"Mommy, where's Bimpe?" she trembled as she asked, forming a fist in anger, waiting to hear it was otherwise.

"She's also at the station with him."

She exhaled, releasing her hard form first before leaving her bed. She patrolled her room, biting her fingernails as her body vibrated in terror.

"So who did he...kill?"

"His pregnant girlfriend."

"Wini...Wini...Winifred?" she stuttered.

"I heard they were arguing and he slightly pushed her but she hit her head on a sharp object and died right away."

She sank to the floor clutching her chest.

"When are you coming to the station?" Mama Rere cried.

She wondered if she had done enough for Winifred at the time.

"You have to come, Folake. Your brother needs you," Mama Rere begged.

She shook her head in disbelief. First she was told off for interfering now she is expected to interfere?

"*Sho gbomi lataro ni?* Come to the station now, we're waiting for you there."

"No, mommy, I'm not coming there," she mumbled, spreading her yoga mat.

"Folakemi! *Iwa ko lon wu yi.* Femi is still your brother and you're the only one that can help him."

"No, he's not my brother," she said firmly. "He's a cousin, and I don't owe you or your sister anything. Tell him to confess to his crimes and accept his punishment."

She ended the call, muttering, "Maybe now, you'll all learn your lessons."

Her first instinct was to call Bimpe, to check up on her since she would know all the details to the story; Mama Rere only called for her help, but never went into the details of how it happened.

"Why now?"

A while later, she tried Bimpe's number. It rang through but there was no response, she tried calling again and this time Bimpe picked up, expressing her fear and faults.

"Aunty Bimpe, it's all my fault. I called her over to discuss issues and he met her there and both fought," Bimpe sounded fraught on the phone.

"Bimpe, calm down. It's not your fault. Are you still at the police station?"

"Yes. Maybe I shouldn't have called the police," Bimpe moaned.

"You did the right thing. How are the children holding up?"

"They are with my parents. We are being held up at the station. The police are assuming I also had a hand in this."

"I'm coming with my lawyers. Wait for me there."

As soon as the call ended, she rushed to take a shower. She didn't take much time getting ready and in about ten minutes she was ready to set out. She had called her legal team to meet her at the police station, instructing them to prepare well to defend Bimpe of the crime she didn't commit.

All she kept thinking about as she drove to the station was the situation on ground - Bimpe and her children. If she had known she wouldn't have left her alone. She would have fought harder for her, thankfully enough it wasn't her that this misfortune befell on. What happened to Winifred was sad and it shouldn't have happened to her if she had stayed away from that toxic man called Femi.

"You came," Mama Rere said, looking surprised and relieved. She was only wearing one slipper and her wrapper was tied outwardly.

Seeing Mama Rere in such a distraught state angered her because Mama Rere had never put so much energy on her.

"Yes, mommy. But I came here for Bimpe," she said, ignoring her aunt who also appeared a mess.

32

Looking back now, Folake could confidently say to her mother and aunt, 'I told you so', because she did.

"If you've listened to me about babying a grown man, maybe you could have saved his life and the one he has now taken," she passively scolded.

Now they were silent, both sisters regretting in silence.

"Please, just help him out," her aunt pleaded. One would think she was the meek type judging by her pitiful expression. She seemed to have gone gaunt overnight and unable to walk straight.

"Aunty, you are at fault. Femi became this way

because of you. You have accommodated every one of his flaws because he's a man, and that is what you're reaping now."

"I know, Folake. I know it's all my fault, but it must not end this way for him. What would the world say about me?" her expressed, dramatically stomping her feet while biting the finger of regret.

She couldn't care less of her aunt's outburst but looked the other way when her mother signalled they both talk privately. She later met with the police officers in charge of the case, Winifred's parents would never settle or forgive anyone for the demise of their daughter, and she only managed to bail Bimpe out, both leaving the station together, while the other women stayed behind.

"You have to brace yourself, Bimpe. The world is not coming to an end. Femi deserves what he's getting," she advised.

Bimpe cried, blaming herself.

"Come on, you know who Femi is, he is never going to change. Killing someone is the gravest crime one could ever commit in this country, and he should be grateful if he isn't killed himself."

"Aunty Folake, what am I going to do now? What will I tell my children about their father? What would the world say about them?" Tears was trickling down her cheeks as she spoke. They couldn't return to their apartment but to her house since the investigation was still ongoing.

The only help Folake could render for Femi was to help him avoid the death sentence, and it was all because of Bimpe's children. They might grow up with their own trauma and disappointment, but sparing the life of their irresponsible father was the least she could do for them.

Few days after Femi's arrest, he was immediately arraigned to court, given a sentence of life imprisonment; he couldn't be sorrowful now for his bad behavior. The following week, Bimpe filed for a divorce and while Femi was in prison both ended their union. If she hadn't stepped in, Femi wouldn't have signed the divorce papers, even though his mother and Mama Rere thought it was a cruel thing to do, she made them realize it was completely over for their dear Femi.

"What a good woman does is to pray every day for her husband's wellbeing, not neglect him in times of trouble," Mama Rere said.

She disappointedly shook her head, feeling sorry for her own mother. "Mommy, you never cease to amaze me all the time. I will continue to pray on your behalf that God will open your eyes to see the light."

Life was getting better lately for her as she was planning ahead for her fortieth birthday, happening in two weeks' time. She was pregnant but had yet to inform Akeem even though they communicated every day. It didn't feel right deceiving him, but if he knew about the pregnancy, he might hurry back home to be by her side, neglecting his own work.

All that was left was the external aesthetics of the airport renovation project, the palace was already down and the opening ceremony was at the weekend. From there, she would pick up Ijeoma and her family to stay with her until her birthday before they relocate to Canada for Ijeoma's PhD study in Survey Engineering.

Getting the Women Entrepreneurship Award had also opened many doors for her, she now dined with kings and the promninent people around the globe. The British Commissioner to Nigeria had also presented an Excellence Award to her for being a role model to women and over her newly found charity foundation. She would also be given an honorary speech at Harvard graduate school in the coming months, and hoped to talk about her life story and journey to success.

"You're trending online," Emma said, rushing into the office with an *IPad*. Smiling, she placed the tablet on the table. "See."

"I hope it's for good this time around?" she asked turning away from her laptop. She had never been a fan of social media.

"Yes. You've even gained more followers compared to before."

"I am on Instagram?" she asked. "How? When?"

"You said to create a PR team and they set social media account for you after the interview with your friend."

She had no idea of what Emma was talking about but it was at the peak of her turmoil.

"So they did a good job," she murmured to herself.

"Of course! They would have been in trouble if they hadn't. Your followers are growing everyday. And they all love you."

"Emma, you know I don't like social media. They are distractions," she said, even though she was moved by the likes and favourable comments.

"Some women said they wish for their daughters to grow up like you, strong and independent."

"They really said that?" she asked doubtfully, but reading it by herself proved that people do admire her courage and lifestyle.

"Some women have even started a single motherhood movement. They want to get pregnant on their own and raise a child by themselves, you have inspired more women in Nigeria than ever."

"But tell them to take things easy, not all that glitters is gold," she warned. Having a child was all she ever cared for in the beginning but now her tune had changed after finding her true love. She was yet to tell Akeem about the pregnancy.

"I think life works miraculously for me," she said,

beaming when the phone rang. She wanted some privacy to speak to Akeem, so she waved Emma away.

Emma nodded knowingly and backed out of her office.

Akeem may have been far, but his presence wasn't. Every week, she would receive a bouquet of flowers sent by a delivery company, his affirmation of love written in a note sent along with it.

"You're spoiling me," she said, gazing lovingly at the bouquet she received over the weekend. Rose flower being her favourite, an assurance of his love for her.

"You deserve more," Akeem said right back. "So, what's new?"

"I want to tell you something," she started hesitantly.

"Actually, I want to tell you something," he interrupted. "I will be coming home to celebrate your birthday."

She gasped and frowned suspiciously. "Aren't you busy?"

"Not really, but I trust my co-founder to fill in for me."

"That's good!" she replied, convincing herself.

"You wanted to say something?"

"Not really, but when you come, you will find out." Although she was grateful to be pregnant with a child at her age, she wasn't sure how he would feel and wondering if everything was happening too soon, she decided to speak to her therapist about it that evening.

"But you don't have any reason to be sad either," Doctor Titi replied.

"I really want this baby, and I want it with him. But what I'm concerned about is his acceptance of the whole thing," she murmured, worried.

"You should trust him to make a better decision. I'm sure if he's the right person for you, he will choose you," Doctor Titi replied.

She couldn't help worrying that she decided to call Ijeoma as soon as she got home.

"I know he's different from the rest, and he's the right one for you," Ijeoma said after she had spoken about her concerns.

She frowned. Ijeoma sounded too sure of the man she had never met before.

"I think it is fate that brought you two together," Ijeoma continued. "It is God's plan that you two met, and he entered your life with ease. You didn't even have to fight it. He was sure and you are also sure."

They were quiet for some time even though her heart was now a tumble dryer.

"You have to let him know," Ijeoma further pressed.

"I will," she sighed.

33

Planning a birthday wasn't an easy feat even though Folake had left it to Ijeoma and Emma to organise. They had invited all the stakeholders, government workers, and her clients, the ones she had worked with. Most of them had RSVPed beforehand, her guest list exceeding over a hundred.

"I still think you should have gotten an event planner to do heavy lifting," she murmured.

"There's nothing I cannot do. All my children's birthday, I planned them all," Emma bragged. "You will have to trust me on this one."

She had learnt to give a couple of her employees the benefit of the doubt because they always exceeded expectations but with type of people coming, she decided to keep an eye on Emma to help where she could.

She looked forward to having Akeem by her side and stopped pestering Emma.

Fortunately, Emma, standing on business, exceeded Folake's expectations. Everything was done to perfection and to match her taste – soft fairy lights glowing above the exquisite floral designs on the tables, the alley and a red carpet motif. She moved to tears when she discovered that Emma had enlisted her design team.

She wore a couture dress, locally made by her trusted designer, the intricate design made it look like she was floating when she walked. It was also the first time she'd let the designer take full control of the desire, and she made a personal promise to reward her. She accessorised the dress with a gold chain and bracelet and wavy-styled cropped hair.

Mama Rere had called some of her friends to attend; thankfully, she and Emma had assumed this would happen. Her peers came out in flamboyant *aso ebi*, matched with *aso oke*, *gele* and *ipele*, Mama Rere felt like the star of the party.

Akeem arrived that day and met her at the venue. He had brought her a thoughtful gift, a puppy she had once asked for, and it made her happier, as the gift was the best one among the rest. She had to introduce him to her mother for the first time, and on the ground, he lay, offering his greetings.

"Ehn ehn, this one is respectful," Mama Rere bragged, showing off her daughter's boyfriend to the her peer, almost dragging him along wherever she went.

She was left speechless by her parent's speech and all the good things they said about her; they weren't the type to praise her, but in her presence, she witnessed their pride in her, leaving tears in her eyes. Everyone who travelled far and wide had something good to say about her. She never knew she had touched many lives and had inspired many. The wife of the state governor, who was a very good friend of hers and had worked with her in the past, raised a toast to honour her, wishing her into her fortieth and many wishes of good things to come for her.

Later that evening, Akeem led a small gathering of family and friends, and in their presence, he went on one knee with a small square box in his hand.

"I know I'm not enough or anything special, but I want you to know that I'll stand with you, love you, worship you, and you will forever be mine," he said, stretching out a diamond ring.

The crowd echoed 'yes'.

She had been too stunned to respond; it was the first time someone was proposing to her.

"Will you marry me?" Akeem asked.

Mama Rere had jumped in as usual, pushing her daughter to accept and not keep Akeem waiting. With her hand covering her mouth, she stretched forth the other hand, accepting the ring and Akeem forever.

"Yes, I will marry you," she said, embracing him for a long time.

"My daughter is getting married," Mama Rere screamed, and others congratulated her.

Akeem lifted her and spun her for some minutes. They cried in each other's arms while Bimpe told everyone she had always known Akeem had a thing for her sister-in-law; Ijeoma said something about 'I told you so', and Emma said she was the matchmaker and that she was the first to know.

"Actually, I do have important news to break to you all this evening," she began after she managed to hold back her tears. Akeem held her hand in his as she continued, "Mommy, Daddy, Akeem, and everyone present tonight, I'm pregnant."

Everyone was quiet for some seconds except Mama Rere who instantly broke into a praise and worship song. Everyone joined Mama Rere except Akeem, who was crying.

"So, we're going to have a baby?" Akeem asked again to be sure.

She nodded slightly, sobbing along with him.

"Yes, it's our baby," she confirmed, tears streaming down her cheeks.

Akeem stroked her cheeks and kissed her gently.

Two months after Folake's birthday, the airport project was launched and the attention it garnered alongside having a share of a late friend's company brought so much attention that the Minister of Interior didn't wait for the launch to be offered to declare her the design for the national museum.

She became a mother to two lovely girls in the UK four months later and got married right after the announcement of her babies and then left for her honeymoon. Being new to motherhood, she got the best help she would ever need from Mama Rere. Their relationship had gotten better.

Akeem had proven to be quite the philanthropist. He expanded his mechanic workshop to take on apprentices. With his analytical skills, he helped revamp her company and her NGO.

With the rapid growth of the NGO, Emma had to take charge of it. A few weeks after her birthday, she learned that Emma had been going through housing difficulties and decided to get her a house on the mainland as a gift. She would have been at the house warming, but a scare had forced her to bedrest.

Global recognition had its mark and being Akheem's wife had the pecks that her awards could never give her, due to her previous experiences with the press, she still refused to grant interviews except once when it was whispered that her school mother's company was about to go bankrupt knowing the interview would draw the necessary attention to the magazine without making her school mother feel indebted to her.

Akeem's start-up company was successfully launched, breaking a revenue gap. He relocated back to Nigeria with his wife and children, both living their best lives while supporting each other's businesses.

Bimpe wrote a biography, which sold out in the first week of its launch after she displayed it on her social media page, became a star and got multiple endorsements.

Ijeoma decided that she was going to be a professor and her husband was in support.

Mr Aleshinloye married her cook, and they still worked with her, but she hired more hands to ease.

A part of her was concerned about how Femi wasn't doing great in prison; he had survived three attacks from other inmates and she feared he might really die there. His mother had become restless, going to vigils and mountains to pray for his release and safety, while Mama Rere had completely abandoned her older sister to focus on her twin grandchildren.

ACKNOWLEDGEMENTS

I want to extend my deepest gratitude to those who've made this book possible.

Agnes Kay-E, my editor. The one who saw the fire in me and fueled my determination through thoughtful feedback and incredible patience.

My big aunt, whose counsel has been my constant strength, nudged me to start and finish this book.

My parents, whose love, sacrifices, and support have been my foundation.

A special thank you to my publisher, Kepressng Ltd, who recognised the potential of my story and has made my dream a reality.

And a most special thank you to all who have, directly and indirectly, contributed to this journey.

OTHER TITLES

Lara meets Lee during a night out. After an unexpected connection, she discovers he is her new boss. Despite their instant connection and her mother's pressure to get married, she's focused on career advancement.

Although Lee is engaged to his best friend to fulfil a family alliance, he is drawn to Lara. He becomes more determined to be with her after he finds out she is his employee.

Out in SPRING 2026